In memory of Ma

Just when I was hoping to hand her the first copy
of this book, my mother, Smt. Kaushalya Mishra, left us

SOCIAL PROTECTION

LANDS OF BLOSSOMING HOPE

Usha Mishra Hayes

PALIMPSEST

Published by Palimpsest Publishers 2020
Palimpsest Publishing House Pvt. Ltd.
16 Community Centre, Panchsheel Park
New Delhi 110017, India

ISBN: 978-93-82622-33-8

Typeset by PrePSol Enterprises Pvt. Ltd.
Printed and bound in India by Replika Press Pvt. Ltd.

Contents

Preface

In 2015, the global war on poverty which had officially started in 2000 with the Millennium Development Goals (MDGs) was further intensified with the Sustainable Development Goals (SDGs). SDGs are significant for two major reasons. First, they are applicable globally. Second, they track all results in keeping with the 'leave no one behind' doctrine. This makes it impossible for governments to hide behind national averages and possible to hold them accountable for demonstrable results and progress among the poorest and the most marginalized along racial, gender and ethnic lines. Remoteness is also a factor. In India, for example, progress in Bastar, one of the most backward districts of Chhattisgarh, will be tracked without being masked by traditional stellar performers like Ernakulam in Kerala. The focus on inequality and accountability bridges existent gaps and is here to stay, and that is definitely good news.

Social protection (SP), key to inclusive growth and development, is defined broadly by UNICEF as 'a set of public and private policies and programmes aimed at preventing, reducing and eliminating economic and social vulnerabilities to poverty and deprivation'. This objective is now embedded within SDGs as a key strategy to help countries achieve the primary goal of 'No Poverty'. With this, social protection can rightly claim success in addressing poverty and concerns about the other basic rights of individuals. It has been further bolstered by the wealth of evidence and data generated recently as testimony to its effectiveness. Over the past 10 to 15 years, the number of social protection programmes has grown exponentially and close to one billion people are now covered by the cash transfer programme in some form or other in 52 countries. Specific child and family benefit programmes, enshrined in legislations, exist in 108 countries. However, despite such visible progress, according to the International Labour Organisation (ILO), only 27% of the world population has any meaningful social protection cover.

True, success has been mixed. Good news is that financial outlays for SP have increased though there is a sharp regional divide among the 36 member countries of the Organisation for Economic Co-operation and Development (OCED) that commit more than 20% of their GDP to social protection or social transfers as opposed to less than five per cent for most of the Less-Developed Countries and low middle-income economies. According to an ILO-OECD analysis, the United Kingdom, without its current level of social transfers, will experience poverty levels as high as 32%, France 30% and in the world's richest country, the United States, poverty would soar to new heights – around 25%.

This book is about the ambiguous, ever-shifting world of policy which influences the social protection systems in select countries in Asia and Africa. It uses an insider's knowledge to examine and dissect the level of interest and assess the drivers and influencers, namely those who occupy key positions overseeing the processing and promotion of social schemes, and identifying obstacles. The book recounts our triumphs and follies – it's about those of us, the indefatigable UN staffers, who have been driven by the zeal of 'making a difference'. It is about our naivety, our errors as well as our drive, passion, perseverance and commitment.

It is a simple narrative largely based on my experience.

Kathmandu
25 March 2020

Usha Mishra Hayes

ONE
Policy Influencing

Predicated on an enabling environment

Policy, for the purpose of this book, will be defined as the basic principles laid down by a government and adopted for its guidance. It encapsulates the declared objectives which a government seeks to achieve and preserve. Policy usually implies a long-term purpose in a given subject area (e.g. land tenure). Sometimes, however, policy is conceived not so much as a purpose-oriented activity but as a cohesive set of responses to a problem that has arisen (FAO 2008).[1] Here policy advice and policy advocacy are used interchangeably.

Policy advice aimed at 'seeking changes in the underlying principles and codes of practice' is a challenging concept. Such changes affect the official superstructure which consists of a coalition of interests. Hence, the resistance to such changes and to policy advice is enormous. Apart from the attempt at fundamental structural changes, policy advice has been defined more broadly as a deliberate process of influencing decision-makers through targeted actions.[2] Policy advice, simply put, requires public action. There appear to be two fundamental aims of policy advice. First, changes in existing policy and then in the way the policy is being implemented.

Effective policy advice is predicated on the availability of an enabling environment. In many cases, substantial policy advice and engagement may need to be committed to creating or strengthening an enabling environment. This requires a focused effort. However, this book is limited to listing some of the key components of this enabling environment as established by a paper from a DFID[3]-supported project which was successfully adopted by the World Food Programme (WFP), the food assistance agency of the United Nations, and other development partners. Set up in 1991, WFP inspired similar initiatives to tackle global hunger. Britain's Department for International Development (DFID) was established in 1997 with a similar mandate: 'to promote sustainable development and eliminate world poverty'.

Bringing about policy change requires an enabling environment, which includes the following[4]:

- A belief that change is feasible, both technically and politically
- Access to policymakers and policy shapers (people inside or outside government who make a direct impact on policy development)
- Appropriate mechanisms for effecting change
- Availability and knowledge of suitable change mechanisms
- Sufficient political will
- A sound research strategy to make use of renewable natural resources

Policy Hierarchy and the Process of Policy Influencing

Policies are multilayered and hierarchical. Acceptance of this fact is important since it helps us understand the challenges involved and efforts required for policy advice and influencing. Policy is embedded within a legal and governance framework and must comply with existing laws. For example, in most countries, the basic framework for national policies lies in their respective constitutions. Then there are various acts and regulations which change and get amended over time. Below that are executive orders and policy statements and finally, standard operating procedures and guidelines. In the area of government-led development activities, there are a host of policies, plans, programmes and projects, each being a little more short-term and specific concerning place and duration than the previous ones, and successively more executive than legislative. As the arm for policy implementation, advocacy groups seeking any change in any of these would actually resort to policy influencing in a larger sense. Also, as changes in plans, programmes and projects generally involve people at the top, influencing programmes may be viewed as policy advice.

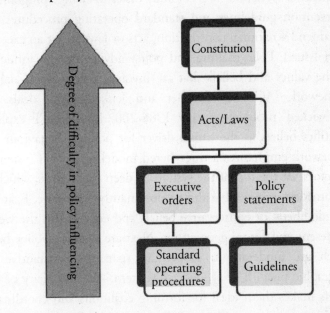

Figure 1: Policy hierarchy and challenges of influencing

The degree of difficulty in influencing groups and individuals increases as one moves up the policy hierarchy. This is not to

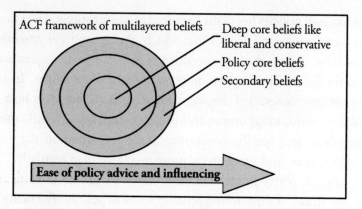

Figure 2: ACF on policymaking and influencing

undermine the hard work and effort required to bring about change at the lower levels, but it is certainly easier to change programmes, intervention guidelines and standard operating procedures than say, amend a national constitution, acts or laws to get an executive order issued. Policymaking and policy advice are also influenced by the values and beliefs that are involved. [Advocacy Coalition Framework (ACF) of Sabatier and Jenkins-Smith deals with the 'wicked' problems during 1988-2007.][5] The ACF explicitly identifies beliefs as the causal driver for political behaviour. The framework emphasizes a three-tiered model of a belief system for its actors. At the top of the system lie deep core beliefs, which are the broadest, most stable and predominantly normative. Examples include liberal or conservative beliefs and concern for the welfare of present and future generations. Next are the core policy beliefs which are moderate in scope and span the substantive and geographic breadth of a policy subsystem. The specificity of such beliefs makes them ideal for forming coalitions and coordinating activities among members. Policy core beliefs are resistant to change but are more likely to adjust in response to verification or refutation from new experiences and information. At the bottom of the model are secondary beliefs. Secondary beliefs are substantively and geographically narrower in scope and more empirically based.

The ACF predicts that secondary beliefs, compared to deep core and policy core beliefs, are most likely to change over time. The experience from PSNP supports the conclusions of this framework.

Implementation Effectiveness and Policy Advice

Policy advice has different objectives as determined by the duration of the programme and its context. As noted earlier, policy advice can influence the formulation of a policy or seek changes in policy/ programme implementation. It can also seek fundamental changes in the policy and even push for a return to the drawing board. That requires sustained, long-term policy advice and advocacy based on carefully collated and credible evidence. While the relevance and role of policy advice at the initial conception stages is better appreciated, it is at the implementation stage that this is crucially required but unfortunately ignored.

The following table presents the possible objectives of policy advice and expected results at various phases of a programme cycle. This is based on the programmatic experience of the author rather than a theoretical framework.

Table 1: Policy advice objectives

Phase	Programme results/objective	Policy advice results/objective
Generation of political will and ownership strengthening the dialogue about the nature and scope of the issue/problem	Define the scope of the programme	Who all need to be targeted and through what programme objectives should be achieved

| Design | A robust design with right targeting, intervention, principles and inputs | Programme inputs and implementation guidelines |
| Implementation | Effective targeting and quality programme delivery to achieve the objectives | Finding the fit between programme objectives and programme instruments including targeting and implementation modalities |

Expanding the table beyond the implementation phase, policy advice can have two key objectives:

- **Change in existing guidelines** as a result of implementation experience to enhance programme effectiveness
- **Change in the current implementation practices** within the given framework for better implementation of existing provisions

The Productive Safety Net Programme in Ethiopia offers an example of achievements and challenges of policy advice in the context of implementation. It underscores the fundamental importance of the established theory: since a programme design can never be perfect the challenge lies in learning and adapting as the implementation process unfolds. This stresses the fact that for effective programming, a continued engagement with policymakers throughout a programme cycle, including implementation, is an imperative rather than an option.

Advice during the process of implementation is often far more important than policy guidance at the formative designing phase, a truism that is often not fully appreciated by the UN and other development partners. This may stem from an inability to recognize the reality of project/policy designing and implementation. Programme managers tend to look at the implementation as a phase rather than one that should be entered into with full preparation and knowledge. Past experience shows that programme implementation or delivery is rarely a one-off task. It is best understood not as a linear process[6] – leading from policy ideas through implementation to change on the ground – but rather as a more circular process involving continuous learning, adaptation and improvement.[7]

In some areas and at times this model works. In some important ways, however, it does not accurately describe the real world that governments and development partners operate in, and its application often leads to failure and frustration. This is because of a variety of factors detailed below:

- **The Utopia of perfect knowledge:** The traditional model assumes that policymakers have complete knowledge about what works. An ideal policy which is fully informed and backed by a solid evidence-base is rarely attainable. Most research gives pointers rather than definitive answers, and in the real world it is not easy to predict how institutions and people will respond. As a result, ideas are tested either in a pilot – with no guarantee that the results can be applied countrywide – or prototypes and pathfinders where policies have to be quickly adapted in the light of earlier experience. In Ethiopia, the PSNF was implemented to scale without any scope for lessons from a pilot. Hence, the need for adaptation and mid-course correction was greater.

- **Hierarchy-induced information asymmetry:** The importance of policy advice during implementation is also accentuated by the fact that decision-makers at the top of hierarchies invariably know less about the operating environment than those on the front lines. This is why in many fields (such as military or business) leaders prefer to use what are sometimes called 'loose-tight' frameworks: a combination of clear objectives and freedom for those with local knowledge to adapt to circumstances. This is very different to the model of 'delivering' a centrally defined solution.

Policy advice, even during implementation, not only enhances the probability and possibility of result maximization, it also provides key inputs and insights for changes. Policy advice should have realistic and focused goals and targets and commit sufficient resources to achieving them. The importance of credible evidence, and a proactive, well-planned knowledge management system cannot be overemphasized.

TWO
Bangladesh

After the soft landing the serendipity factor

In Dhaka on a sunny vibrant day in the summer of 2004, a few colleagues from DFID and WFP learnt another meaning of 'social protection'. Its tenor and scope charged with swirling emotions and deep values were as powerful as 'human rights'. We all felt inspired. It had the right flavour, imbued with the concepts of protection and social values, as opposed to mere economic ones. It immediately closed the gap between patronising 'hand-out' policies and the accountability of the state in protecting its citizens. All of us involved in the programme were moved by the warm, comforting feeling it evoked. We who work in the field of social advancement are perpetually on the lookout for more effective solutions – if not silver bullets then silver linings.

Dhaka was teeming with a multitude of humans, a large number of deprived street children among them. Social protection as an idea and a campaign theme caught our fancy. This was something that we could show off at Gulshan and Baridhara, the city's exclusive clubs where diplomats are regulars.

However, for the term to gain traction it had to be given currency in the policy circles of Bangladesh's capital city. In essence, we had to get the government equally excited about social protection. Leading this introduction drive was the World Food Programme (WFP), quickly joined and even outpaced by the World Bank and their Human Development advocates. The idea of social protection thus found a home. In GDP and monetary terms, Bangladesh was, and is, one of the poorest countries in the world. But it is immensely rich otherwise – in culture, heritage and the warmth and love of its people.

Dhaka has incredible creative and intellectual resources. Bengalis love their music, poetry, paintings, dances and theatre. This is the country of global thinkers and economists who have given the world the concept of micro credit. Nobel Laureate Md Yunus' Grameen Bank[8] brought in an easy, informal banking experience and an NGO culture that helped the rural poor escape the stabs of extreme poverty and vicissitudes of periodic political upheavals by ensuring availability of basic education, healthcare and livelihood. In the 2006 UNDP Human Development Report, Bangladesh was mentioned as a country with human development indicators defying economic essentials.[9] In 2018, its HDI value was a comfortable 0.614, putting the country in the medium human development category. Between 1990 and 2018, Bangladesh's HDI value increased from 0.388 to 0.614, a 58.3% increase, and it is now one of the best in South Asia, ahead of India and Pakistan.[10]

For the ever-inventive development brigade, the idea of social protection was an easy hook, coming as a refrain soothing to the ears. In the world of policy influencing and advocacy, sometimes things come together fortuitously, some out of deliberate, conscious effort and some as a sheer coincidence. These are all important to the policy process. Policies are made, shaped or changed initially in the minds of key influential thinkers of a country. The United Nations provides a great platform to these movers and shakers.

In early 2004, the terms which were being bandied about, those closest to the idea of social protection, were social safety nets, poverty reduction and, interestingly, food security. The essential idea of food security was best understood within the government. Whenever any such idea reaches a government it is referred to the ministries and agencies responsible for protecting the vulnerable segments of people from starvation and ensuring that their nutritional status improve progressively. Among them is the Ministry of Finance, most clued in on social and economic policymaking by virtue of its being staffed with some of the smartest officials. It is this ministry which opens the coffers or decides otherwise in the time of mass starvation and deaths. Finance Ministers are often at the forefront of driving the basic food security policies with the focus being understandably on availability and access to nutrition.[11]

For Bangladesh, which was hit by famine soon after its birth in 1971, food security was important. The country maintained 600,000 MT of food reserves, much to the chagrin of some UN agencies, a reminder of the tragic fact that often there is no perfect congruency between the pat solutions of the UN and the concerns of a host government. In fact, quite often there are sharp divergences of opinion, views and positions. A government in a crisis situation tends to be guided by its political concerns instead of acting bold which involves risk-taking. It's the role of the development agencies then to step in to hedge these risks or demonstrate the scale and feasibility of some of these pat solutions that they are keen for the governments to roll out. The record of such interventions is patchy at best, hence the emphasis on innovation in our respective country strategies.

We all understood the crucial importance of food security but could not promote the concept in its entirety. Social protection provided a new lever for promoting food security. The economic access to and dimensions of food security offered a strategically important and useful hook for social protection, an idea whose time had come.

Driven by its newly-acquired ambition of influencing various multilaterals, including the World Bank, DFID had just launched an innovative partnership with WFP Bangladesh. Inherent in its overall vision was a move to transform WFP into a development agency from an organisation predominantly reactive and responsible for relief and emergency responses. DFID funded three senior advisory posts within WFP Bangladesh. The programme, the DFID-WFP Partnership Agreement (PA) as it was christened, lasted for over three and a half years and turned out be to be transformative not just for WFP Bangladesh but for WFP globally. The project had three distinct though interconnected arms: policy, disaster preparedness and knowledge management. The portfolio of food security and social protection fell in the ambit of policy.

When the DFID PA started in the middle of 2004, it met with the usual institutional resistance to change and to new ideas as well as to new advisers, who were all selected from a non-WFP pool of candidates (a DFID conditionality) with an underlying assumption that only outsiders could challenge the status quo and bring about necessary changes. The project was slow to start and took a while to find its niche. Eventually, the policy arm started to tackle critical national interests like food security, a Vulnerable Group Development Programme and social protection. Food security had injected the development discourse with the crucial concept of 'economic access'.[12] It was not enough for food to be available in the market. It was equally important that the households had the necessary financial means to buy food. Social protection ensured that access. Though as a concept it was much wider than just food security, it was the availability of basic food and regular income giving one the purchasing power that encouraged the government to tackle the problem at its roots. It realized that either the families needed a regular income to buy food or food had to be distributed for free. It was not difficult to appreciate that they also required money to meet other basic needs like clothes, education and health. Bangladesh already had some cash and a few kind-based programmes on, targeted at the poor, economically vulnerable, orphans and widows.[13]

In early 2005, the World Bank in Bangladesh commissioned a stocktaking of the social safety nets in the country. It was a staple WB exercise serving a useful purpose of collating the outlays on various social safety nets and social welfare programmes in one document. The largest of these social safety net programmes, Vulnerable Group Development (VGD), benefitting 700,000 women from ultra-poor households was being implemented by the Ministry of Women's Affairs and WFP. A largely food-based programme, it was run as part of the Income Generating Activities (IGA) with microcredit thrown in as a graduation element. The IGA training progressively expanded to include other elements like reproductive health, nutrition and HIV-AIDS awareness.

The programme was widely perceived as hobbling because of mistargeting and leakages. The World Bank was one of the fiercest critics of food aid in Bangladesh. For its part DFID while opposed to food aid favoured a wider debate on the issue in the public space and within the government as well. WFP was left holding its breath. Nonaction was not an option. Among the various other measures, WFP had already commissioned a leakage study and was working closely with the government to plug the loopholes. But food aid was problematic not just on account of leakage. It was proving to be costly apart from depressing the market and dampening the producers' incentives. The DFID supported WFP and its Policy Adviser, took the issue head on and instituted a major research on the efficacy of both food and cash in enhancing livelihoods of the most marginalized.[14] That research helped WFP in several ways but most importantly in demonstrating to the Bank and other development partners that WFP was open to questions even if these went against an organization's founding principles. WFP Bangladesh, fully supported by its Rome Policy Division, was showing the way for the global organisation. Details of this radical transformation of the UN agency's mission are an important sidebar to the main story, which had a lot to do with the story of social protection in Bangladesh.

The WB report had exposed the embarrassing fact that despite a multiplicity of social safety net programmes in Bangladesh, only a very small percentage of the most vulnerable had any effective coverage. In 2005, out of a population of 147 million, with over 30% below the poverty line, less than five million had access to any social safety net and almost none to any predictable, reliable and sufficient social protection. The rate of poverty reduction was poor with natural disasters neutralising the impact of steady economic growth. The idea of inclusive growth and equity that guided the UN agenda over the next decade was still a work in progress. Social protection was introduced against this backdrop of development and poverty challenges. The change in strategy turned out to be strategic and timely.

PPRC (Power Participation Research Centre) is one of the finest NGOs and research agencies in Bangladesh headed by Hossain Zillur Rahman, a very influential thinker and researcher.[15] WFP approached PPRC with a specific proposal: partnership and support in organizing the first social protection conference of Bangladesh. The WB which was also in talks with PPRC over a host of developmental issues, learnt about this and offered to come in to join forces with WFP. The two engaged with PPRC jointly and decided that a national social protection workshop would be jointly organized by the three agencies. Thanks to the excellent rapport Hossain had with the General Economy Directorate (GED) of Bangladesh, the government, the most important stakeholder in the discussion, came on board, closing the circle.

GED was headed by a visionary and outstanding civil servant of Bangladesh, Dr Mesbahuddin Ahmed. An economist by training, he had worked with the Ministry of Finance and Economy and was a champion of pro-poor policies and programming. He was deeply respected at the UN quarters as well as by local civil society including BRAC (Building Resources Across Communities), a prominent NGO, and Grameen Bank. GED had the responsibility for drafting the first PRSP[16] of Bangladesh for which they had commissioned PPRC. The inclusion of GED ensured that there was an express link with the ongoing national development policy thinking. The social protection idea now had a strong possibility of being mainstreamed, perhaps much sooner than anticipated. This was a fortuitous development not planned and conceptualized by WFP. The World Bank may have seen this coming but the links which proved to be the most enduring and a strategic contribution to the conference, had not been immediately clear, proactively explored or sought after by WFP.

The conference which WFP conceived as an event of national importance, evolved into an international one thanks to the zeal and resources of WB. True to their modus operandi in such affairs, the Bank flew in a battery of international experts from Washington setting the tone for a high-level meet. The two-day conference ended with the decision to create a placeholder policy for developing PRSP.

In terms of attaining its policy objectives, the conference was successful, laying the ground for further policymaking and identifying the key contours of a social protection agenda for Bangladesh. Subsequent developments were slow but steady with the other UN agencies, especially UNDP, stepping in to provide UN-level leadership. In 2011, Bangladesh was ready to define its social protection strategy. It had taken about six years for the policy process to mature from the opening deliberation of 2005, experiencing several programmatic shifts, evolutions and expansions. The policy was meant to cap endeavours like the introduction of an employment guarantee scheme and free health vouchers as well as expand scholarship and food assistance programmes.

In 2011, when I visited the country to present inputs on child-sensitive social protection, the country was grappling with issues of coverage targeting, graduation and financing. The Ministry of Finance was central to these discussions. There was a pronounced emphasis on disaster mitigation which again was extremely relevant for Bangladesh.

State of Social Protection in Bangladesh

Going by the latest accounts, the country is finalising plans for reforming its social protection system. Since my observations pertain to 2016 or before, they are still valid though relevant figures might have slightly changed over the past few years. A paper available from the Planning Ministry which details the scope of reform, projects a highly ambitious outcome with far-reaching implications. Should Bangladesh actually go this route, it will be one of the first developing countries to have systematized a social protection mechanism and implemented it to the letter.

At the core of the vision statement or futuristic plan is a proposal to overhaul the existing system by the mantra of consolidation and optimisation. It promises to do away with the bane of the existing social protection process: multiple uncoordinated programmes transferring inadequate benefits. It also grapples with the problem of institutional arrangements, with the focus on creating a new Ministry of Social Development as the nodal ministry for implementing all social protection schemes and programmes. The ministry is tasked with setting up a register of eligible persons and households as well as implementing a result-based Monitoring and Evaluation (M&E) programme, including a robust appeal system. The plan appears to be guided by the best global practices in social protection. Whether this gets implemented or is diluted or even scuttled will only be evident with the passage of time, but the vision and the policy process have certainly attained maturity.

Recapping Lessons

The lessons learnt from these developments and programmes are crucial to formulating future plans and policies and can be summed up as follows:

Policy influencing requires a driver going after a clear, specific policy goal. Such a central figure then becomes the driving force behind agglomerating other forces and resources and creation of an enabling environment, provided the next steps are correctly identified and properly planned.

The next steps are dependent on an anchor point to kick-start national policy thinking. Initially the national policy does not have a countrywide focus but is still being discussed with some select players, influencers, decision-makers and practitioners at the national level. However, it often acts as a catalyst to transfer a thought or an idea on to the national-policy stage.

At this stage it is vitally important for the UN agencies and the WB to join forces. It helps the programme tremendously. The WB typically brings in more substantial resources but the UN provides more programmatic, practical, in-field experience and a psychological ease of operation. This is mainly because senior policy staffers are often based in the country and have access to the government. Also useful are the partnerships with local offices of the international NGOs, research firms and other national, civil society entities. It almost always boosts the programme. This merely requires a couple of meetings to share ideas and facts and to bring them up to date on policy opportunities and a demonstrated openness to receive their inputs. Often policy-shaping and influencing are done on the basis of such simple tools and techniques. Though huge in reach and impact, it is the simple things that often carry the day for a UN policy advocate.

The key lesson is about knowledge, or about how knowledge gets used. As Francis Bacon famously said, 'knowledge is power', in some cases it also becomes an enabling factor to access the influencers. It is important to establish a partnership in which the task of producing and sharing knowledge is not seen and undertaken as a favour or demonstration of superior intellectual prowess but as part of one's fundamental duty.

The next lesson is regarding the choice of alliances and champions. This is perhaps the single most important factor. The allies should be drawn from both government and civil society.

It is important to establish a broad alliance based on mutual respect and genuine concern for the country's wellbeing, the distressed and the most marginalized. Few people will be unwilling to support a person who has the best interest of their people in their heart. This sounds simplistic but some of the most effective approaches and strategies are the ones that are generally the simplest and most direct.

A key lesson is that policy influencing is an unglamorous, tedious, extremely slow-moving task. One has to be committed to the long haul. The result which impacts the lives of millions of people is worth the wait and perseverance. It is only the slow and steady that wins the race. There are simply no shortcuts.

The other lessons are about what could have been done differently. In order to answer this question, one needs to revisit the policy environment and the realistically defined policy space available to the UN and the WB. Typically, the WB is the policy heavyweight in a country with the UN playing a supportive though extremely important role in the areas of poverty reduction and social protection. This has not changed much since 2005.

Clearly, even to the most important policy influencers or shapers, there was no policy space available outright, it had to be carved out. The introductory workshop was able to hit all the right targets but this was not sustained by a comprehensive initiative to influence policymaking on the part of WFP. The agenda was pushed subsequently by UNDP which took on a leadership role and managed to bring along the WB and other UN partners.

PPRC continued to support the research and policy dialogue around this agenda and gradually social protection gained currency. This is evident from the developments in the country as I recollect them. The lessons serve as pointers to the agencies that take on a lead role in the reconstruction of the country devastated by periodic cyclones and flooding.

Policy influencing should be seen as a marathon rather than a 100-metre dash. As long as the momentum is sustained and the engagement of the right actors ensured, a UN agency should not be bothered about competition for the leadership position. It's not part of its culture to enter the race. Nor would such an agency spend its resources on such trifles.

Last but not the least, it is important to reflect on things done and targets ahead. This calls for an extremely rare capacity to be self-probing and self-critical and always questioning the means and the intermediate ends. In many ways, this could be helped by the latest tools in the classic Theory of Change. A systematic Theory of Change developed for any policy goal will help unearth several hidden assumptions and identify strategies for converting them into winning actions.

THREE
Ethiopia

From memory of national pride to famine to fabulous growth

Coming to the distressed landscape of famine-struck Ethiopia, the obvious question that confronted policy wonks like me was why another overarching policy framework was required particularly when the mammoth Productive Safety Net Programme (PSNP) was already on.

PSNP is an international flagship programme both in its scope and partnership approach having reoriented a rural safety net to respond more effectively to the needs of food-insecure households and make productive investments to underpin rural economic growth and environmental rehabilitation. This is achieved through: (i) predictable provision of adequate food and cash transfers to targeted beneficiary households, thus allowing effective consumption without any asset depletion; and (ii) creation of productive and sustainable community assets that contribute to the reclamation of severely degraded areas and boost household productivity.

In 2003-04, faced with the need for sustained relief,[17] the Government of Ethiopia (GoE), in partnership with the donors, embarked on designing and implementing the Productive Safety Net Programme (PSNP). Launched in 2005, the PSNP was the outcome of a comprehensive exercise to establish and foster a partnership between the GoE and a coalition of donors. Among them were nine major donor agencies: CIDA, DFID, EC, Irish Aid, Netherlands, SIDA, USAID, WFP and the World Bank.

This was one of the most ambitious initiatives in Africa, second only to the launch of the Child Benefit Programme in South Africa which was initially opposed by its Finance Minister and could be launched only with the intervention of President Mandela who announced the measure without prior consent from his cabinet.

Ethiopia took a quantum leap in social protection and moved in this direction much against the advice of its key development partners following the example of Malawi and Lesotho earlier. For those familiar with Ethiopia's history and culture, this should not come as a surprise. Ethiopia, despite persistent famines and massive poverty, has remained a proud nation. Ethiopians are keen to point out that they are the only people in Africa that had resisted colonialism. Ethiopia had remained unconquered by the Europeans through the centuries when most of the continent came under the yoke of ruthless colonialism. Its assertion of independence stemmed from a sense of unity, a study by political scientist Jacob Hariri of the University of Copenhagen points out. Therefore, the country has been unvisited by problems that assailed most of Africa. It was unaffected by the enervating experience of colonialism that not just drained a country economically but sapped its confidence and self-esteem as well.

Though the country successfully avoided external subjugation, it was largely under authoritarian rule until recently. The Marxist-Leninist military junta of the Derg that had captured power in 1974 and ruled Ethiopia for thirteen years was finally challenged and ousted from power in 1987 in the aftermath of the devastating famines. The junta leader, Mengistu Haile Mariam, sensed the popular resentment against military rule in the aftermath of more than a million deaths in the horrible famine and the debilitating war that wrought havoc with the country's economy as well. Ethiopia was finally on course moving towards stability and economic growth.

When pop star Bob Geldof, horrified by the famine in Ethiopia, conceptualized Live-Aid, a multi-city concert, fundraising got redefined. Apart from raising £111 million Live-Aid put famine-relief prominently on the diplomatic agenda and inspired other charitable efforts including Red Nose Day.

Meles Zenawi who took over as President after the fall of the Derg junta, later became the country's Prime Minister. A dictator to the core behind the façade of democracy, he practically wiped out political opposition. After nearly 200 people were massacred at an opposition rally by government agents, no semblance of political dissent existed in Ethiopia anymore. In the 2010 general election, Meles' EPRDF won an absurdly high 99.6% of Parliament seats leaving only one for the opposition and another for an independent.

Meles focused on growth even as he eschewed democracy. Starting with a low base, the country progressed on to attain a GDP growth rate of nine per cent by 2002 and sustained it. Other indicators too improved significantly making Ethiopia one of the rising stars featured in *The Economist* cover story: 'Africa

Rising' in December 2011. Poverty had declined by almost two percentage points between 2004-05 and 2009-10, reducing from 38.7% in 2004-05 to an estimated 29.2% in 2010, according to the Ministry of Finance data. Between 2000 and 2010, the human development index (HDI) for Ethiopia improved by an annual average growth rate of 2.73%, from 0.250 to 0.328 – making it the third fastest growing economy in the world since 2000. Primary school enrolment had climbed from 33% in 1992 to 95.9 in 2010. Overall, there was a clear shift towards pro-poor investments with an increase in the share of total expenditure directed at spending on poverty-targeted sectors from 42% in 2002-03 to over 64% by the end of 2007-08.

PSNP supports over seven million people who face severe food insecurity, and has made significant achievements promising even more. By resorting to cash transfer and addressing the basic consumption needs, it has helped avert extreme hunger and also built household resilience for a sizeable number of people. The programme encourages investment in assets and opposes the tendency to make a distress sale of assets (Hoddinott, 2008).[18] There is a clear vision for graduation at the end of a five-year programme cycle through provision of complimentary inputs like credit, training and agricultural extension. With an impressive budget of $2.1 billion (2010), PSNP remains one of the largest, most ambitious initiatives in programming through partnership on the African continent till date.

The donors have pooled their resources in a World Bank-managed trust fund that provides direct budgetary support to the government. Interestingly, the donors provide a food channel to the famine-stricken population and at the same time they are part of the same unified budgetary framework for a single government-led programme orchestrated by the Food Security Coordination Directorate (FSCD) in the Ministry of Agriculture and Rural Development (MoARD) of the GoE. All the partners have agreed and they strictly adhere to a unified stream of technical advice, monitoring and evaluation.

This alliance, called the 'New Coalition for Food Security', established a multi-sector technical group including the government, UN, donors and NGOs. WFP was an active and vocal member of this group not only because of its leading role in emergency response but also due to its experience and success with the MERET[19] project (which was recommended at the Copenhagen Climate Change Summit 2009, for adaptation and replication across the globe) in addressing the livelihood risks faced by those most vulnerable to food insecurity. Following the work of the Coalition, a group of donors (the World Bank, the EC, USAID, DFID, CIDA, IrishAid, WFP) agreed to come together to assist the government in developing PSNP to build food security by specifically addressing livelihood constraints and bolstering the most vulnerable section's resilience to shocks.

The group also brought a big focus on available knowledge surrounding social safety nets coming out of the World Bank (the theories that are now part of the broader social protection paradigm). A Donor Working Group (DWG) was established, supported by a team completely dedicated to coordination. The Donor Coordinator was assigned along with the rotational Donor Chair, to establish mutually acceptable positions within the group and be the main interlocutor with the government. All the partners agreed to let their individual views be subsumed by the collective opinion.

The objective of the Coalition was to develop a strategy to make targeted interventions by building on existing successes and scaling up initiatives struggling to take off given the obvious constraints. The PSNP assumes crucial importance for the Ethiopian economy: its budget constitutes about 1.2% of gross domestic product (GDP) – almost as much as the allocation for health in the country's budget, at 1.4% of GDP – and about 62% of total *woreda* (district) expenditures in PSNP areas (World Bank, 2009).

PSNP was a massive response from the country's leadership determined to change the distressing picture of people starving and dying due to recurrent droughts. It was meant to counter the kind of temporary band aids applied to this human catastrophe that had hit Ethiopia regularly over the past decades.

PSNP expanded and spread out rapidly. It was essentially a food for work programme with the difference that it focused on the poorest and the most arid districts of Ethiopia for the six months of the non-agricultural season. There was an additional component of rations for labour-deficient households or those too weak, old or disabled to work on PSNP projects. By all counts this was a strong and effective response to the challenges of food insecurity and starvation, the foremost social problem faced by Ethiopia for which it had come to portray the tragic image of serried skeletal figures dying like flies. In the context of PSNP the challenges of implementation were as serious as that of design. Due to the rather forced nature of a jointed approach by the key donors as well as the government and others, there were many issues unresolved and left pending.

While a consensus was built on the principles of PSNP early in the design process, translating them into a detailed programme design – from its size and targeting methods to the types of transfers and mode of payment – was, at times, contentious. Because of difficult circumstances, incomplete information, conflicting views and competing interests that were never fully resolved during the design process, implementation had been severely affected and compromised.[20] Resolving the issue required continued engagement of the partners including the GoE.

When it comes to development and the harsh realities conditioning it, there are neither any model programmes nor ideal designs. Even the best of the programmes when replicated, plays out very differently as it intersects with a different set of policy priorities, interests and the dynamics of various groups. All this influences the way programmes are understood, adapted and implemented. A programme or policy design is not merely a technical issue. It is an outcome of a largely non-technical process involving negotiation and iteration among a range of actors. Technocrats and financiers are just two major interest blocks or stakeholders' groups within the government.[21]

If the designs are not perfect, necessary decisions cannot be made and negotiations and trade-offs are postponed. The value of policy advice during the implementation phase is more than at other times. Also, because the UN does not have any direct control over the external environment in terms of decision-making as it works with governments, people in general and civil society in particular are sought to influence the policy direction. It is vital for the UN to recognize the importance and centrality of influencing decisions through civil-society interventions throughout the project cycle and especially during the implementation phase.

PSNP provided the right model of a quantum leap without the perfect design and ideal preparation. What PSNP was keen to unleash was an idea, a belief that it is possible to mainstream relief within a development agenda. The centrality of this belief can be traced to anti-dependency sentiments and a government which favours a minimal state and greater resilience and self-reliance of communities it serves. Consequently, it was against a hand-out approach. Such a belief was in keeping with the growing emphasis on DRM (Disaster Risk Management) where the chronically poor, who form the majority of relief beneficiaries in any emergency, can be supported through developmental interventions to graduate from acute poverty into self-sufficiency and resilience. In this context the Advocacy Coalition Framework (ACF) of Sabatier and Jenkins-Smith (1988)[22] that emphasizes the importance and intersections of beliefs and values in achieving policy shifts, is useful in explaining the new initiatives marking the transformation from emergency relief to a reliable safety net. The following table maps the various beliefs and values for the government, donors and PSNP.

Table 2: PSNP values and beliefs

Beliefs	Government	Donors
Deep core beliefs	Anti-communist with conservative flavours	Humanitarian support with a do-no-harm motto.
Policy core belief	Anti-dependency, conditional transfers	Varied, conditional and non-conditional transfers. DRM stressing mainstreaming of relief within developmental interventions.
Secondary beliefs	Targeting the most vulnerable, implementation of productive public works and natural resource management	Food or cash, duration of the support, mainstreaming gender and the marginalized.

As is clear from the above table about adaptations within PSNP, there was significant congruence of beliefs among governments and donors at all levels. A major shift in the belief system occurred at the core policy level where the donors' concern about the conditional transfers as exerting an unnecessary burden on poor households, and the government's fears about dependency, were addressed through an affirmation of non-conditional direct support for those who could not contribute labour.

This programme had fully involved most of the national and international development partners. The WB, DFID and other bilaterals had committed substantial resources. WFP was bringing in food but was also a recipient of resources for supporting implementation of the project. Ultimately, it was a massive food aid programme.

   In the initial years of the project, there was not much support for a social protection policy. Gradually, as PSNP matured and lessons were learned in the field, the process and programme became more reflective of the ground realities. Huge numbers of people were still left out. Everyone could not participate in a work-related programme and those left behind, needed year-long support and not just for six months which PSNP planned to cover through 'take home ration'. In addition to foodstuff, cash was required to meet the other needs of a household. Moreover, there was an increasing challenge of urban poverty, an area PSNP was not involved in. With several vulnerable groups not covered by PSNP, there was a danger that several groups would be left without any support. The need for an overarching social protection framework was a clear recommendation from the international development community.

Among the multilaterals, UNICEF was leading the charge for a social protection framework with the WB, WFP, IGAD and select INGOs (international NGOs) as committed supporters. A social protection working group had been established at MoLSA (Ministry of Labour and Social Affairs) which had started to meet weekly just as I joined WFP. WFP agreed to a $300,000 partnership with MoLSA to support policy development. An overall policy framework was needed to address the SP issue.

PSNP had made the country more ambitious in terms of addressing the challenge of economic and social poverty. Its success in staving off starvation and famine had certainly boosted the government's confidence and made it believe that some seemingly intractable problems could indeed be addressed by direct, deliberate actions, and that there was a developmental solution to a developmental challenge. This was a confident and resurgent Ethiopia that was being persuaded to adopt a social policy framework.

As far as the government's engagement was concerned, it started with a single agency. But this single agency was also the patron and owner of the mega PSNP. Hence, it carried huge clout. The director of the ministry was an upright, compassionate and dedicated person who had been holding talks with the international partners and had learnt to be suitably assertive as well as engaging and encouraging. He was supported by a very able and committed deputy armed with excellent interpersonal skills.

The advocacy for a social protection policy called for the development of alternative supplementary approaches. Cash transfer was one such. Cash had steadily emerged as a viable option, a lesson learnt from the tsunami of 2004. The World Bank's loss of confidence in food as a mode of relief spelled an existential threat to the World Food Programme. The concept of periodic, predictable and unconditional cash transfers was very new to Ethiopia but was built around the lessons learnt from PSNP where a sizeable section of labour-deficient households had failed to get sufficient support.

WFP food distribution point in Rangpur, Bangladesh: assisting the Vulnerable Group Development Programme, the country's largest social safety net. Women receive monthly food support for two years along with six months of training in an income generating activity and access to microcredit on completing the training. The programme ensures protection as well as promotion of rights of some of the poorest women in Bangladesh.

Women turn up in their best at WFP food distribution centres: a poor person seldom wants to flaunt poverty. Social protection programmes enhance this deep, inalienable sense of dignity and self-respect by placing resources directly in the hands of individuals and within a rights-based framework. In a modern, accountable state, social protection is seen as a right of citizens, often guaranteed by Constitutional Provisions, rather than a charity from the state.

Boys and girls in Chittagong, beneficiaries of WFP-supported School Feeding Programme. Vitamin and mineral fortified biscuits are distributed among primary school children in food-deficient districts of Bangladesh. The programme provides the much-needed calories and nutrients to children enhancing their enrolment, attendance and retention.

Inside a WFP factory where high-energy biscuits are made for distribution among primary pupils in some of the poorest parts of Bangladesh. High standards of quality control have been made possible by training rural women in essential sanitation, hygiene and production processes.

Despite having a high pace of urbanization and one of the fastest rates of poverty reduction, Cambodia retains its rural charm and also boasts of an increasing expansion of social services like health, education and roads. Still dependent on natural, renewable resources, combined with modern equipment and machines, Cambodians have strategies for sustainable living.

Since 1991, when the Paris Peace Deal was signed reconciling the perpetrators of genocide with the communists backed by Vietnam, UNICEF has supported millions of children to finish basic education, building human capital in a country that was bled and brutalized by the Pol Pot regime. Such interventions help counter the iniquitous growth that divides Cambodian society down the line.

The author: at the shrine of eternal love in the Kaole ruins, Bagamoyo, Tanzania. Hundreds of tourists visit the UNESCO heritage site which is also an extension of the Tower of Livingstone, a fabled Catholic church.

A big day in their lives: schoolgirls welcome a UNICEF delegation in Iringa district, central Tanzania. The conditional cash transfer programme impacts the education scene dramatically raising school enrolment.

With literacy touching their lives, the young girls look forward to a better future. The new thrust to education in the UN-sponsored social protection programme with cash transfer as a key element has changed Tanzanian society in many significant ways.

In this 2015 photograph the author is on her way to Charkent in a UN armoured vehicle. Many senior UNICEF officials spend a larger part of the day traversing through the dangerous Taliban-controlled areas.

Part of the forbidding Afghan landscape: an abandoned Russian tank on the plains of Mazar is now circled by blushing violet flowers making it look inconspicuous.

A UN armoured car returning from Charkent

In the summer of 2014, a Pashtoon boy recites from his grade 4 book at the community-based school supported by UNICEF in Charkent. These are the only schools available in remote parts of the country. The social protection pilot is aimed at transferring a small but regular amount of cash support to families to help them send their children to school.

The author at the centre discussing key programme features in the office of the District Governor, Charkent.

The first recipient of funds from the cash transfer programme for women uses her ATM card. Among those present is the Provincial Governor.

The little 'uns coo: colourfully dressed Afghan girls sing at the launch of the UN-sponsored cash transfer project in Charkent. The strong demand for more such projects across the province is a pointer to people's aspiration for a new beginning.

Photo credits: the author and some of her UNICEF colleagues

There were other important lessons around the child-related outcomes. According to some of the evaluations, prevalence of child labour in the PSNP households increased as did school absenteeism with the children being pulled out of school to do household chores. This enabled their mothers to work on the PSNP projects to boost the family income which was severely inadequate. In their attempt to attack a problem the women seem to have created another.

An overarching social protection framework was prescribed by the international development community. Some of the agencies, not members of the PSNP coalition, were equally keen to ensure social protection coverage for their demographic target groups. For example, UNICEF was keen on social protection for children while UNAIDS was worried about those battling HIV-AIDS. Everyone wanted to be part of a mega project while PSNP was unable to accommodate all of them. A strident call was given for a Social Protection Strategy. Of all the voices raised UNICEF's was the loudest and strongest.

There was also the challenge of sustaining the programme. It became increasingly evident that most of the households would continue to need support for the foreseeable future. Participation in the programme helped stave off starvation but did not result in meaningful poverty reduction. PSNP, in hindsight, performed quite well in protecting the most vulnerable segment of population from the stabs of extreme poverty and also, preventing the occurrence of famines scarring the marginalized who were particularly susceptible to scarcity. This programme, however, had no 'promotive impact'. Let me explain the term in detail. When a new method or experiment in any sector is tried out experts look for any long-term or permanent outcome. For example, a new chemical spray for plants saves a crop from insect attacks and moreover ensures a bigger harvest. While protecting the extremely poor from the assaults of famine, PSNP, however, did not have a far-sighted objective to pull people out of poverty.

This was an insurmountable hurdle before the programme. The challenge segued into policy advocacy for a social protection framework. Ethiopia's uninterrupted seven-eight per cent GDP growth rate in the recent years provided a strong and comforting backdrop to the discussion on social protection. The conversation around the integration of graduation elements like microcredit was gaining a new momentum. It was increasingly accepted that the monitoring-and-evaluation frameworks needed to integrate with, and not just impact, food security, income, children and development outcomes as well. Those dealing with women's issues had to be more systematically mapped, monitored and responded to.

The frenetic pace of urbanization and its inevitable corollary of poverty with children begging openly on city streets threw an urgent challenge to the policy planners to reckon with. This unplanned, unregulated and relentless growth was cause for concern. The government was keen on starting a social fund, a throwback to Ethiopia's socialist past. They had a project document put together by a doctoral candidate that they wanted the donors to buy into. The proposal had an instant and spectacular appeal as it conjured up an image of beggar-free streets. The Ethiopian first lady was especially keen to see the ungainly sight of beggars jostling at traffic lights wiped out. However, a more humane approach would always be more desirable and morally permissible. A social fund backed by private patrons, the government and (hopefully) development partners would give communities an opportunity to design local projects providing meaningful engagement to the poor and vulnerable and in the process contributing to the social and economic infrastructure of the area.

The international donors were, however, not enamoured of this approach. Such a fund, they reckoned, would fail to provide protection to those who needed it the most. Being controlled by the local community and the government, the fund would be prone to misuse. Such approaches had become largely defunct and were being steadily replaced by nationally backed, resourced and predictable social protection programmes like cash transfers.

The need for drawing a clear-cut outline of an overall framework was becoming more urgent by the day. It was also obvious that the government would require orientation towards capacity building. An overall social protection framework was still in its infancy. One of ILO's seminal programmes had contended that a basic package of social protection would require at the most eight per cent of the GDP. There was also a larger consensus around addressing the needs of poor vulnerable children. In Livingstone in 2008, the African nations had committed to what came to be known as the Livingstone Accord, pledging up to two per cent of the GDP towards the wellbeing of vulnerable children with social protection instruments. The national advocacy was attached to some of these regional hooks and commitments. Plus, there were other stakeholders that needed to be covered, with the elderly and persons with disability being at the front of the queue.

The government was not averse to such an approach and the Ministry of Labour and Social Affairs (MoLSA) appreciated its relevance. Though it would be some time before the larger government apparatus got pulled into the debate, MoLSA served as a powerful and strategic driver. PSNP gradually spawned a whole policy and research architecture which in its turn formed a think tank and laboratory for policy direction. The WB and other partners set up what came to be known as a social protection coordination group. Its task was to support coordination with line agencies and also to commission research and studies. The idea was to push attendant advocacy to effect necessary changes in the programme with the help of the government.

The WFP-organized workshop proved to be the first largescale initiative at building a baseline of understanding for such a framework. There was participation from all levels. IGAD had also started implementing a small but important project on formulation of a social protection strategy for Ethiopia with consultations at both regional and state level. WFP and other partners helped amplify that effort manifold.

Social Protection in Ethiopia

Today Ethiopia has a strong social protection system comprising developmental, disaster management and emergency responses, prioritising the poor and vulnerable, aiming to expand new instruments like insurance and maintain traditional ones like food security programmes. The policy fundamentally is comprehensive, addressing both demand- and supply-side constraints with four pillars:

1. Social safety nets
2. Labour and employment benefits
3. Social insurance and
4. Reduction of inequities in accessing basic social services

Tying in reducing economic constraints by measures like fee waivers with the physical access to basic services through measures such as 'adapting physical infrastructure to the need of the physically challenged' and addressing capacity constraints through training institutions, by expanding and building the capacity of the social welfare workforce. The policy in many ways transcends some of the jejune shibboleths around demarcation between access and availability of social services with a clear focus on the purpose, reflected in its mission statement: 'To see all Ethiopians enjoy social and economic wellbeing, security and social justice.'

PSNP today gives predictable support to over 8.3 million chronically food-insecure households. By making predictable cash-and-kind transfers it has helped avert hunger and build household resilience for a sizeable portion of the participants. It allows investment in assets and discourages distress sale of assets (Hoddinott, 2008). There is a clear vision for graduation at the end of the five-year period through a provision of complimentary inputs like credit, training and agricultural extension. Budgeted at a total of $2.1 billion (2010), PSNP remains one of the largest, most ambitious efforts in programming through partnership on the African continent till date.

The cash donors have pooled their financing in a World Bank managed multi-donor trust fund that provides direct budgetary support to the government. The food donors have channelled this separately but it is part of the same unified budgetary framework for supporting a single government-led programme, coordinated by the Food Security Coordination Directorate (FSCD) in the Ministry of Agriculture and Rural Development (MoARD). All the partners have agreed and they strictly adhere to a unified stream of technical advice and monitoring and evaluation. Such a strong unitary trend, many of us would recognize, is rather rare among the development partners.

Ethiopia teaches us that strategies can spin out from the experience of implementing programmes. Countries should get busy with what is needed most. In case of Ethiopia what was required was a predictable safety net or a social protection programme that would shield people from the adverse impact of drought in the first place. There was an urgency to build resilience and mitigate the blows of chronic recurring droughts. That was the national priority. The government had no time for debating, drafting and finalizing policies. It was a relief operation with a difference – the relief being provided six months in advance and by enhancing opportunities of earning enough before drought crept in. The programme also helped the communities with water conservation and build management structures to shore up irrigation. Development partners, therefore, had no need to clamour for effective strategies. This eventually led to the realisation that an overarching strategy was of utmost importance. What was important was to get started on the path of social protection. Opportunities and challenges along the way would mandate responses requiring an overarching framework and sometimes programmatic revision.

FOUR
Cambodia

From a bubble to a wave, from mere agenda to national priority

As a participant in the relay race of policy-influencing I arrived in Cambodia at the tail end of a process involving adoption of the social protection strategy by the Council of Ministers.[23] This chapter deals with the trials and tribulations of getting an idea translated into budgeted plans offering enhanced coverage and support to the vulnerable population.

Cambodia is charming. Despite its recent history of war and genocide, the country has been able to regain its mystique as an ancient, enchanting place providing a peaceful, comforting home to a majority of its 14 million people. Prime Minister Hun Sen, one of the longest-serving leaders in the world,[24] has been able to ensure stability and growth during his rule since 1985. However, democracy is the first casualty of stability. Democratic only on paper, it is actually more akin to a 'benevolent' dictatorship. Despite its many shortcomings and failings, Cambodia has succeeded in two important areas. First, uninterrupted stability for 35 long years underscores the coercive power of the state and Hun Sen's wide acceptability. Second, it has brought material progress. Cambodia has pushed poverty almost to a negligible level. On the poverty alleviation front, it has achieved one of the most impressive rates globally[25] – from 19% in 2011 to 11% in 2014.[26] Even on non-monetary poverty, the country has made significant progress. HDI improved from 0.544 in 2010 to 0.566 in 2016. From the donor viewpoint, the synergy created by democracy, development and political stability has created an efficacious growth environment. While Cambodia's limited democracy should cause concern, one needs to bear in mind that the country struggled to emerge out of a dark spell of war and horrendous episodes of mass killings. The award-winning film *The Killing Fields* recounts the worst excesses perpetrated by the Khmer Rouge regime. The stunning recovery of Cambodia gains significance in the light of failures in Pakistan, Afghanistan, Iraq and more recently Egypt and Libya.[27]

Cambodia for a long time had opposed social protection much to the annoyance of the donors and development partners. Like many other countries it, too, initially saw social protection as a hand-out inducing dependency. The concept did not find much resonance within a larger national ethos that emphasized karma[28] or the sum total of one's life as the outcome of actions. Sufferings and deprivations were explained in terms of karma. So, a person's misfortune, according to this school of philosophy, is their own making and not the result of an unequal and exploitative social arrangement. The issue of political culture in the country seldom receives the necessary attention.[29]

In 2011, Cambodia which had buried the ghost of Pol Pot long back, was firmly set on the growth path, committed to attaining the Millennium Development Goals and Sustainable Development Goals. A free-market proponent, more importantly it was part of the most effective and efficient economic zones – ASEAN.[30] The social protection policy acquired a new dimension for Cambodia in the wake of the 1997 Asian economic depression. Beginning July 1997, the financial crisis that gripped both East Asia and Southeast Asia raised the spectre of a worldwide economic meltdown. Precisely at this point the role of the state (along with that of planned development) was reiterated.[31] Almost a decade later, the global economic downturn of 2008-09 triggered by the food, fuel and finance crisis – the Triple F crisis for short – created a strong policy opportunity for the advocates of social protection. In Cambodia, the economy had contracted by three to four per cent raising the level of poverty and distress significantly for the first time in a long while. Faced with such severe challenges, countries often come up with mega policy responses.[32] The Development Partners (DPs) had used that space well and worked the Council for Agricultural and Rural Development (CARD), the agency responsible for social protection policy. CARD had worked with the DPs to draft an SP policy adopted by the Council of Ministers.

This was an important achievement made possible by a strong collaboration between the DPs and CARD, especially in a region where till 2014 the social protection coverage was one of the poorest. The entire process had lasted over two years and involved 100 plus meetings.[33]

After adoption of the policy, CARD and Cambodia came to be seen as leaders in social protection in the ASEAN region, a part of the world which had a greater underspending on social protection than say, Sub-Saharan Africa and even South Asia.[34] It was a turning point. CARD started being invited to conferences around the world to present the strategy and the process of social protection. Cambodia basked in the glory of being one of the first few countries to have an overarching, life-cycle based, cutting-edge social protection policy. The unmistakable stamp of agencies like ILO, UNICEF and the WB on the policy was for everyone to see.

It also provided a useful reference point for CARD to advocate resourcing social protection schemes. Efforts here are to trace the struggle to get a strategy translated into budgeted plans leading to enhanced coverage and support to the most vulnerable sections of the population. This proved to be more challenging and disappointing than initially anticipated.

In the euphoria following the adoption of the policy there was a palpable confidence about a progressively expanding social protection coverage. We were soon proved wrong and the policy success was followed by months of disappointment and disillusion set in. The WB sought to persuade the government to launch a cash transfer pilot that would aim to make available monetary incentives to poor households with children below six provided they agreed to accept certain health and education conditionalities. These missions made no significant headway for almost three years. The factors impeding progress included concerns over design, the benefit size and extremely narrow targeting. The real reason, however, was the continued suspicion of the Ministry of Finance about the usefulness of social protection. This, many would recognize and agree, is one of the toughest problems encountering those advocating rapid expansion of social protection coverage for the most vulnerable. This was the situation prevailing in 2011. The picture has most certainly changed over the years and resistance to SP has significantly gone down creating a more responsive environment in which SP has come to be integrated into the Sustainable Development Goals.

However, Cambodia had incorporated elements of the SDG into its policy framework even before the UN launched the Goals in 2015. Though getting the MoF on board has continued to be a nagging problem, the country is more open to the concept. The lessons from the process and events leading to securing the engagement of the MoF is, therefore, extremely relevant.

In hindsight, getting the strategy approved was far easier than it would have been in many other countries. However, a government's commitment to a policy is tested more by its readiness to resource it and the quality of implementation than mere adoption. The worst abuses are perpetrated by some of the countries that have the most progressive laws and policy framework. Paraphrasing TS Eliot,[35] one can contend that 'between policy and implementation falls the shadow' or in this case, the 'policy implementation gap'. (see Chapter 1)

In many ways, the factors leading to successful policy formulation also contributed to its poor uptake – one of the abiding ironies of policymaking and policy influencing, especially where donors appear to be strong and (often dominant) players.

The first was a humongous donor interest and donor push. All the key players including heavy hitters like the WB, UNICEF, WFP and UNDP came together to work with CARD to draft the strategy. There is important and credible evidence to suggest prevailing vulnerabilities, and the new drivers of change as well as existing social safety nets and their inadequacies were compiled and factored into the formulation. The engagement was consistent often calling on specialized, focused resources underlining both donor interest as well as their commitment. This support was strong and unwavering.

The second key factor was participation of the Government of Cambodia. Here it is important to elaborate on the term 'government'. Many policy and advocacy documents use the word 'government' rather liberally, even erroneously implying that it is like an unwieldy, awkward creature – hydra-headed with many hands like an octopus, a behemoth with multiple echo chambers. To some others, it is a unidimensional and single-minded monolith that moves in unison and therefore, needs to be engaged as one entity. The reality is often far from all this.

In Cambodia, within the government structure, the Council for Agriculture and Rural Development (CARD) is an important power centre. Though technically not a full-fledged ministry but a council, it is headed by the Deputy Prime Minister and reporting directly to the Prime Minister. He is ably assisted by the Secretary General. The fact that the Deputy Prime Minister headed CARD underlined its singular importance. This route comes in handy for getting a programme or strategy approved by the Prime Minister, the most powerful voice within the Council of Ministers. In those days when I was there it also helped that the Deputy Prime Minister's son was married to the Prime Minister's daughter. Ironically, these two factors also contributed to the poor uptake of the policy.

While donor interest is vital in pushing an agenda, an excess of it can overshadow the realities of political economy and even displace the need for a national discourse. In this context, 'national' implies a broad, inter-sectoral and multilayered approach rather than one engaged with a single agency. This is an important distinction.

Policy-influencing suffers from a unique problem, one that the downstream supporting service delivery system is generally shielded from. For reasons which are more historical and institutional, when a donor tries to promote or introduce a new policy, it is assumed by the government that they have an 'interest', which, to a bureaucrat often translates to 'dollars'. This stems from their experience in traditional, downstream aid. Governments are still not used to development partners playing a truly selfless role in helping a country formulate a sound, flawless policy. No credible government will offload the responsibility of policymaking to an international agency consisting of foreigners and expatriates who they rightly gauge to be far less informed than they are. However, governments do often agree to lead and partner with DPs on policy formulation in the hope that the new policy will attract additional donor interest. In this process, control of the contours and objectives and scope is still firmly in the hands of the government. Seldom will the concerned ministry and departments agree on policy elements which lack overall ideological and political alignment with the larger national ethos. The government will go to great lengths to ensure that everything that is sensitive and against the prevalent political leanings is kept out.

The space then made available to the international partners turns out to be one of strictly technical support, of producing global evidence and best practices and providing answers to the government's questions. The partners provide coordination and secretarial support. Governments welcome analyses and evidences, documents and reports. They even seek support in getting a first draft together and then sift through this from their own perspective, choosing some and discarding others.

That is ownership steering as would be recognized by many. This brings me to the second factor driving the successful adoption of the Cambodia strategy, which also imperilled its implementation. However social protection, an inherently cross-sectoral agenda, also needs a cross-sectoral buy-in. Hence, government ownership needs to be more broadly defined.

Initially, the ownership of the strategy was neither sufficiently deep nor wide-ranging. That proved to be a huge stumbling block for the next stage of policy advocacy, getting the strategy programmed, resourced and implemented.

The challenge was to deepen and expand that ownership, in essence pushing social protection higher up the agenda so that it became the business of the government and central to its growth strategy. That should be the vision – the dream policy agenda for a UN staffer – calling for an all-out persistent effort requiring both knowledge and diplomatic expertise to influence decision-makers. From a close reading of the existing literature it is clear that this leap of logic is not difficult to support.[36]

Today the issue of growth is no longer a simple one of numbers and variable factors. Governments have increasingly come to appreciate that growth needs to be inclusive. This implies that the primary task of the advocates of social protection is to demonstrate how it promotes inclusive growth. But before that it needs to be established that SP promotes growth through quantitative impacts.[37] While the latter is indeed a huge plus, I would contend that in light of increasing currency for inclusive growth, an advocacy that pins SP to the inclusion agenda stands a high chance of success. Moreover, the strategy that impacts the overall growth rate is far more potent than one which focuses only on inclusion.

Generating this evidence proved to be the lever that helped deepen and broad-base the ownership of the newly adopted strategy and brought it to a more central position in the national-policy thinking, programming and eventually, budgeting. Generating evidence is a fantastic opportunity for establishing the credentials of the agency involved and also for reinforcing deeper, more trustworthy relationship with the relevant stakeholders. The significance of this development should never ever be missed or minimized. Evidence research is not just an academic exercise; it is an important influencing opportunity for the UN, and for an advocate to engage the government in a policy process.

In Cambodia, the task of making SP central to growth-related thinking and the engagement of stakeholders in generation of evidence could be made through a dialogue with the powerful Supreme National Economic Council (SNEC), a think tank for aiding the Prime Minister and the Ministry of Finance in their vision. It was headed by the Finance Minister and its Deputy Chair was a very capable, amenable and upright politician, Dr Hang Choun Naron.[38] In its economic thinking and strategic planning this agency was an ally of the WB. However, their involvement in social-protection discussions was negligible. This gap offered us an important and potentially transformative opportunity.

The challenge was to gain access to an agency that had hitherto been involved only with issues related to hardcore economics. Its staff consisted of some of the smartest economists of Cambodia. And their job was presenting complex economic models to the Prime Minister and Finance Minister on a daily basis. That was where social protection needed to penetrate.

Along with SNEC, there was yet another more impregnable fortress, the Ministry of Finance. Humourless and pragmatic, they were solely concerned with GDP growth rates. They could not be influenced much with issues such as equity, inclusion and resilience. They were there to ensure that the books added up as neatly as possible and that the country averted any major economic disasters. In other words, they cared solely about economic growth and avoiding any fiscal traps. They made the budgets and parcelled out the money but that was done in a mechanical, pragmatic way rather than with any ideals. GDP growth for them was a more compelling reality than social conscience. Budgeting traditionally had been incremental rather than results-based. But this arrangement was in a state of flux.

UNICEF faced a daunting task of making this ministry appreciate and support the agenda of social protection. The agency needed to initiate, orient and guide the finance mandarins into a programme from which they had largely been kept aloof so far. This was a serious gap in previous policy advocacy efforts. But then, in a relay race, the task of the baton holder is to advance the race rather than bemoan the shortcomings of the previous runner.

It is often assumed that policy-influencing is based on an explicitly detailed strategy. The reality, however, is not that simple and very rarely does a detailed Theory of Change or a logframe underpin a policy advocacy process. While such a strategy is certainly not devoid of any serious thought or method, it is also not as tightly predicated on a project plan as is service delivery intervention.

This proved to be the case for Cambodia as well. While clear anchor points for the next phase of policy advocacy were identified, initiating the process took many twists and turns which were not entirely scripted. Whether such processes can or should be entirely scripted cannot be said with any confidence.

UNICEF then conceived of a study titled 'Estimation of Rates of Return on Social Protection Instruments.'[39] This was the turning point. It transformed SP from a predominantly social agenda to an economic one and provided a lever to start engaging with the MoF and SNEC.

The policy was impregnated with other important opportunities. Cambodia was just unfolding its ambitious VISION 2030 as well as a five-year National Strategic Development Planning. It was imperative that social protection was incorporated meaningfully within these processes and the final documents. Failing this, the strategy would remain very much a pet project of a single agency and its donors, lacking political and economic teeth and traction.

National allies again proved to be game changers. This group was again an extremely well-respected and credible voice just as in Bangladesh.

Access to SNEC was secured through this ally. As in Bangladesh, it was the national angle which when leveraged, proved very effective. This should be a sobering realisation for the UN expatriate community. Host governments almost always have more time for us if their national thought leaders evince interest in our work. Otherwise, unless one goes to a country with huge personal, academic and intellectual capital in terms of reputation, one is still a mere UNICEF/UN staffer to be replaced in due course by another. Seldom have I seen government officials being influenced by the intellectual prowess or brilliance of the UN diplomatic staff. The UN certainly does not recruit or retain such intellectual giants. Such luminaries are best found in academia.

Mr Chan Sopha I,[40] chair of a leading national research agency, was approached by UNICEF for broader research collaboration. It is also possible to reach out to such people and institutions for guidance and ideas. Often these are kindred spirits appreciative of any request for analytical inputs required for working out a strategy or arriving at the big picture. The engagement strategy was broader than just social protection. Starting with social protection might appear too sudden or outlandish for the MoF or SNEC; hence a cautious approach.

For the MoF the entry point was capacity building on programme budgeting within the ministries UNICEF had a close working relationship with. The MoF valued this support especially as it was in line with their current priorities and also because it conformed to the larger reform agenda being pushed forward in partnership with the Bank. This was also supportive of the coordination role that the MoF is mandated with.

Partnerships between ministries can at times come under strain due to differences in approach or a power tussle among the concerned ministries and ministers. To circumvent this, the MoF usually appreciates the role of a helpful outsider. This capacity-building partnership provided opportunities for a broad-based dialogue which soon came to include social protection linked to the growth agenda. Indeed, the broader partnership had more elements than can be presented here. It is enough to say that starting with simple capacity-building support, UNICEF emerged as a partner of choice for the MoF which approached the UN body for several of its pioneering, small-scale but high-impact investments. UNICEF had the good sense and judgement to support implementation of some of these strategic activities, which went a long way in demonstrating that the UN agency was an empathetic and understanding ally.

The finance ministry began to be regularly invited to key UNICEF meetings and events. And they quite often turned up despite being always super-busy. Despite the fact that UNICEF was nowhere as big as the WB, at a launch event of Phase II of the Public Financial Management Reforms,[41] the Head of Cambodia UNICEF was the only UN Head of Office on the podium along with the WB, SIDA and EU, despite UNICEF's contribution being less than one-tenth of the smallest donor's to the PFMR kitty.

With SNEC again, a broader partnership was crafted with the help of several research papers linked to human capital accumulation and inclusive growth. Though only a few of the activities were finally carried out, it helped UNICEF forge an acutely strategic relationship. I have already recounted the role of credible national partners. In this case, it was Chan So Phal, the CEO of the National Economic Policy Research Institute, that helped introduce research activity.

With the 'Rates of Return' (RoR) study, the advocacy and partnership with NEC and other line ministries started to shape up. SNEC, a deemed partner in research, provided the team with national accounts data. This study helped create an economic aura around the socially-oriented UNICEF and made the Bank and other agencies including the IMF take note.

ASEAN Moment

Policy advocacy efforts can often benefit from an unexpected international or regional development. In 2012, Cambodia became the chair of ASEAN. This grouping of 10 Southeast Asian nations, essentially an economic bloc, was busy setting regional benchmarks and standards in areas like decent working conditions, climate change and so on. Multilaterals including UNICEF and ILO were in discussion with the regional blocs for long-term partnerships. UNICEF, for example, was on the verge of entering into a partnership for promoting child rights and child protection throughout ASEAN. The concept of partnering with ASEAN was not something new. However, all these partnerships had been conceived and were being forged by the respective regional offices in Bangkok. When Cambodia became the ASEAN president, UNICEF Cambodia mooted the idea of partnering with ASEAN on social protection. Such a leadership role on a regional issue from a country office was new, and as it turned out, not all that foolhardy.

Beginning 2015, ASEAN was set to become a strongly integrated economic bloc, with the member countries agreeing to an unrestricted, visa-free movement of labour.[42] Such mobility of labour presented a unique set of opportunities and challenges. There was a need for ameliorative and protective measures so that all could benefit economically and ensure that the vulnerable populations of the member nations were protected.

To me this was the ASEAN moment. It was not conceived in the UNICEF office, though the UNICEF staff had a role in its making. The compound where I lived in Cambodia was also shared by a senior World Bank official, Enrique, and a UNDP colleague, San Jose.

We often found ourselves together in the swimming pool chilling with our children. The concept of inter-agency advocacy around a social protection framework for ASEAN was born at those informal meetups. Three of us discussed and agreed that situating social protection as a mechanism for promoting integration with a human face was the right thing to do.

The Cambodian government was thinking along similar lines though we were unaware of it. When I met the Deputy Minister of CARD later that week, he chuckled mentioning that he was thinking exactly about the same issue. He was enthusiastic and committed to using the opportunity of Cambodia's chairmanship of the regional grouping to push for an ASEAN Social Protection Framework. Cambodia organized the first ASEAN conference in Seam Reap in 2013.[43]

A whole new chapter can be written on this regional ASEAN process of integration but it is enough to say that Cambodia's assumption of regional leadership boosted national advocacy initiatives and helped the country's social protection agenda climb up the national policy priority list and consciousness ladder faster than would have otherwise been possible.

A few key points need to be reiterated here:

Against the backdrop of the social protection initiative, what emerged with abundant clarity were a few important lessons for shaping a policy process at the implementation stage.

1. Situate the policy within the larger national planning and policy processes.

2. Links with the Ministry of Finance are of critical importance. Linking the policy and strategy to the growth agenda and priorities could be a huge boost.

3. Evidence generation is an opportunity for partnership and advocacy. Plan it well to broad-base the engagement. Involve the MoF and other key ministries as peer reviewers and key stakeholders.

4. Situate social protection as far as possible within a broader circle of supporting resilient and equitable growth.

5. Forge a bond with local influencers to help them facilitate new partnerships and alliances. Overall, our goal should be an empathetic, understanding partnership.

6. Last but not the least, seize on regional and international hooks to lift the national advocacy agenda.

Social Protection in Cambodia, 2016-17

The latest news travelling from Cambodia is that the country recently passed a Social Protection Law. This is the climax of all initiatives on the policy-development front. Social protection finally became a justifiable, permanent feature of law giving this sensitive area of activity protection from the whims of executives and politicians. The journey was not only sustained but progressively accelerated as well. Prior to this, the vision of social protection had been integral to the five-year national development plan and VISION 2030. All the key ministries and agencies finally understood and appreciated the role different provisions of the social-protection law could play to safeguard and empower vulnerable sections of the population, provide them access to development opportunities and help them reach their potential. The country, which had reduced poverty dramatically over the past decade, also witnessed a manifold increase in investments towards social protection.

Along with policy formulation, the legislation put firmly in place all its key elements. Cambodia's Ministry of Planning maintained a register of marginalized, vulnerable and therefore, eligible households for the IDPoor[44] programme. In terms of coordination and institutional arrangements, CARD was in the leadership position with the advantage of being able to report directly to the Prime Minister. Signature programmes like the Health Equity Fund and School Stipends met the targets set for them although the country still needs to take a decision about the relevance of a cash transfer programme like Mexico and Brazil have. That may not happen anytime soon but other development opportunities and outcomes are already being promoted for an increasing number of poor and vulnerable households. As a concept social protection in Cambodia is on firm ground, especially after acquiring the recent legal teeth. It presents an inspiring model for the other least developed countries (LDCs) and lower-middle-income economies.

FIVE

Tanzania

On familiar ground, social protection set to flourish further

Tanzania was an uplifting experience where social protection seemed to be already at its peak when I arrived. A largescale cash transfer programme had been in motion for the past two years. There was no need to further stress the relevance and importance of social protection. The government, persuaded by the WB and other major development partners like DFID, was already convinced. The task at hand was more about enhancing the effectiveness of the programme and making it more responsive as well as efficient. Importantly, the programme had started undergoing revisions acquiring more refinement in the first phase itself. Only those changes perceived as incremental and not too disruptive were made. The programme was indeed implemented at an incredibly fast pace.

At the same time concerns were raised particularly by UNICEF, WFP and a few other agencies like HelpAge about the inadequacy of coverage. There were also issues concerning the availability of social services like health and education for a programme of conditional cash transfers. The government's willingness to raise the level of its commitment to the programme was duly noted by the donors. On the basis of this renewed engagement, a demand was made for an overarching social protection policy that would help address many of these issues.

There were several players in the field who came together to support the cash transfer programme of the Tanzania Social Action Fund (TASAF). The programme, targeting the extremely poor households, covered about seven million people, transferring anywhere between 10 and 15 dollars to a household that had school-age children. TASAF also had an interesting component – an unconditional base or top-up transfer for accessing education and health facilities. The programme expanded in phases while enrolment and targeting were in full swing. The aim was to cover 1.5 million households across the country within two years. The administrative and logistic challenge of achieving this in a relatively low-capacity environment was not well appreciated in general. The timeline was tight and detailed. The government stuck to its schedule as monitored by the WB and other development partners. Regrettably lessons from the implementation experience were not exactly learnt and acted upon. The programme had no space to deal with any scope for mid-course refinement at the management level.

UNICEF too had growing concerns. The key one was lack of integration of nutrition into the programme. UNICEF felt that a fantastic opportunity to raise the nutritional status of children was being wasted. The UN agency would have liked to maximize the results from the conditional cash transfers and felt the 9-16 age group should have been integrated into the programme. UNICEF would have preferred to turn TASAF III into an ECD (Early Childhood Development) plus cash transfer programme. This would have been very much in line with the recent lessons from across the world that the ECD agenda formed the bedrock of any social protection programme. Investments in childhood in the early stages enhance cost-effectiveness of the social protection programmes and augment human-capital outcomes.

However, the target audience was rather diffused. There was not just one person or institution; there were many and they were a varied lot. In this particular case the number of agencies and stakeholders that needed to be lobbied and influenced were exceptionally large. There was of course the chairperson of the TASAF management unit. More often than not they would direct us to the WB which in its turn would refer us back to TASAF arguing that this was a government-led and owned programme. This is, regrettably, a situation encountered in several countries. Often, government agencies position themselves behind the donors in order to avoid taking a stand while the latter put the onus on the former. This in the process heavily burdens the task of policy influencing. The crux of this strategy is reaching out and establishing contacts.

The World Bank in Tanzania had a strong presence and the social safety net programme was headed by a group of experienced and amicable international staffers. That was the front end of the WB. The backend and resources could be traced to Washington, which thereby added a whole new twist to the challenge of getting the WB on board. This then extended to convincing the UNICEF HQ in New York to join the programme.

The WB has its own cycle of programme implementation. There are quarterly monitoring sessions in which UNICEF and other development partners participate. These are important occasions for sharing evidence and issues in a systematic manner and UNICEF is committed to making the most of these meets.

UNICEF's advocacy position was helped tremendously by the fact that it was also the coordinator of Tanzania's Social Protection Working Group. In hindsight, there was not any policy agenda that I could not promote. The results were often substantive. The main outcome was the success in influencing the process, thereby enhancing the quality of the dialogue and the evidence base. Often, given the amount of time that one has to spend in a country, the best approach is to be direct and straightforward while taking care to be humble and being able to project genuine concerns for the country and its people.

In Tanzania, sharpening the focus on the ECD component of TASAF required sharing of information and lessons from across the globe. However, mere sharing of knowledge and evidence would not be sufficient. Partnership with the government to implement a pilot project integrating many ideas and components required both time and patience. Such a scheme makes a strong demonstration effect and boosts the government's confidence in its feasibility and about the need for its replication. It becomes aware of its own capacity to adopt a new approach. This is not to discount the influencing that one still has to do to convince the government about the pilot. A pilot seeking to influence a country's policies and programmes should, as far as possible, be implemented with the participation of the government deploying its human resources. Designing such a project is a sure way of influencing and capacity building and its importance as an initiative cannot be overstated.

UNICEF launched its pilot in select targeted districts and used the access to share knowledge and evidence from such programmes globally. The situation in Tanzania was favourable to such moves. It was a very opportune moment for any work related to social protection. One of the key factors behind the success of the agencies and DPs in promoting the agenda was the leadership of the Permanent Secretary in the Ministry of Finance. He was a senior bureaucrat with a refined outlook and, significantly, a former Director of TASAF. While he now had a much larger remit, he remained a passionate believer in social protection and a pro-poor policy orientation. The Minister of Finance was also the co-chair of the Technical Working Group on social protection. This was fortuitous for the social protection agenda in Tanzania, an opportunity often not available in other countries. In fact, getting the attention and involvement of the Ministry of Finance is one of the toughest challenges faced by the agencies in many parts of the world.

Here in Tanzania, the most powerful civil servant in the MoF, Dr Servacius Likwelile, had the experience of working in this sector; a former TASAF Director, he also headed the Technical Working Group. It was indeed a coincidence that threw up an excellent opportunity. His deputies and other members of the team were also deeply committed. The Deputy PS, Policy, an academic, was largely engaged in helping his boss with social policies. By virtue of this access, the normal stages of policy influencing were done away with. Prioritization was vital to the programme. However, mainstreaming social protection remained a challenge. The MoF had, in theory, a coordinating role, but the line ministries and directorates often lacked the capacity to appreciate and integrate social protection in their policies and programmes. Familiarity with the details of the programme and their implications was evident in the country but it was still very limited, not widespread. More and more children were being covered under the programme but the number of teachers did not go up proportionately, raising the prospects of deterioration in quality; an increasingly sensitive issue for UNICEF.

The health sector faced similar challenges. The problems on the ground assumed greater proportions but were yet to be duly recognized, systematically addressed or acknowledged by Dar es Salaam, the capital. There was a gap between the reality and experience on the ground, action requirement and corresponding response from the authorities. Selection of beneficiaries was based on an unnecessarily complex model, combining geographical, community-based targeting and Proxy Means Testing. This ensured a high level of accuracy though the errors in exclusion seemed to be glaring which was no surprise given the high poverty levels. It was difficult to separate one poor household from another. Unless social protection was offered strongly and uniformly, the targeting, it was realized, would appear arbitrary or biased and the coverage inadequate. It was a crucial moment for Tanzania.

Complaints were mostly about the inadequacy of coverage. TASAF III heavily depended on a strongly motivated community cadre as well as a district-level unit. Selection, verification, monitoring and mobilization were all carried out by the various community-level committees. The CMC, or the Community Monitoring Committee, which had a key role, was the backbone of the programme. Ensuring quality implementation depended on two key factors. First: awareness of the entitlements of the programme and participation. Second: access to the services. The first phase of this conditional cash transfer programme met the two basic criteria as a measure of its success. This was a practical approach for Tanzania given its capacity, size, terrain and other complexities. However, the CMC needed more knowledge and awareness. Lack of such inputs could seriously undermine programme performance and, by extension, future support.

Given the ambitious rollout and the very strict targets set, UNICEF's advocacy priorities were being steadily conditioned by feasibility. Also, it did not lack in strategic intent. Mainstreaming social protection and slotting it within other cross-sectoral policies and programmes, like the Five-Year Plan (Mukukuta and Mukukuza) and the provincial and district plans, was a very important, strategic move towards social protection. The concepts of a national strategy for growth, poverty reduction and human rights are appropriately captured in the Swahili words *mukukuta* and *mukukuza* used in naming the programme. The timeframe for the campaign was 2011-2015. Along with the ECD, it became the second prong of UNICEF's advocacy efforts.

The second goal required a much larger, multilayered initiative across the sectors. Here the vast pool of experience that UNICEF had at its command came in handy. Its advantage was it operated in all the key child-relevant social sectors, and deals with the appropriate ministries and departments for implementing successful, conditional cash transfer programmes. The overall ambition was to ensure that social protection became everyone's priority.

Social Protection For All

While we try to build ownership pacts externally, forming a coherent internal alliance with various sectors is both challenging and crucially important. The difficulty has a lot to do with the silo mentality displayed in approaching programme implementation. The vertical silos are headed by subject experts who have sector-specific results to achieve. That consumes most of their energy. This suggests a problem with the framework of results and the theory of change analysis, or even the strategic planning exercise. Increasingly, a muted demand and lack of financial and economic access are perceived as major factors in perpetuating deprivation affecting the social sector – a high rate of school dropouts and poor nutrition. Important supply side factors condition the growth of the sector. Despite recruitment of teachers and enroling of students, school education has been dented by poverty in a much more menacing way than is often recognized. The child is pushed out of school to work to add to the family kitty. As a result, they are deprived of the free uniform and nutritious food served by the school as part of the midday meal programme. This slide impairs the family's motivation to achieve self-improvement, move upward socially and economically. The psychological impact of poverty often gets overlooked and does not feature in policy conversations. The impact is visible in different aspects of the community's life. Deprivation raises hurdles for the underprivileged to improve the quality of life.

Often the factors that prove decisive are physical and therefore palpable and countable. In most developing countries, with sectors faced with a huge supply gap, the decision-makers are understandably focused on the numbers game. The situation has begun to change with UNICEF giving a new priority to the quality of education. Even a casual analysis of the factors contributing to poor completion rates brings out other issues like student-teacher ratio, quality of teaching, teaching material and the impediment of poverty. What makes the situation even gloomier is the child's own willingness – under family pressure and whacks of poverty – to work earning a little instead of going to school. It is here that social protection serves as an effective intervention motivating the child to prefer the classroom over work, thereby paving a better future for them. Strengthening the demand for education among children and their families as well is a major challenge for the agencies involved.

If the sectors involved appreciated this more than they currently did and accepted the role of poverty in deprivation, their enthusiasm for social protection would have been more robust. Often, we do not think long-term and about strategic factors. We programme and act on targets that we can meet within a short tenure of three to four years before moving to another country for the next posting. This is a criticism not levelled against individuals but points to a limiting factor in aid programming. People involved in framing social policy have their own blinkers and inadequacies. A key factor impeding progress is lack of aptitude. We usually are more academic and research-oriented, quite often trained in economics and tasked with situation analysis and environmental scan. We tend to think of ourselves as smarter than others. The fact remains that our understanding of the ground reality is only knee-deep.

That certainly is a serious drawback, the inability to make expertise useful for the team at large. Tied down with our own assignments and other responsibilities, it was all the more difficult to pass on the knowledge. A third factor is that the success rate of the programmes would be different had the theory of change been properly constructed and the role of poverty and its ameliorative strategies better understood. In normal situations, when a team is working from one deadline to another, and the senior staff are more worried about Annual Performance Goals, inter-sector results are the immediate casualty.

If our initial efforts fail to evoke an enthusiastic response or are snubbed, we tend to retreat into a shell. We fail to recoup and seize the initiative again by restrategizing and marshalling our resources. In the process we become far less useful to our counterparts in the country's government than we would have been otherwise. A realization sips in that it is more important to get it right within UNICEF than one assumes. While this calls for overhauling our system and a realignment of priorities and policy dimensions, we are not the only ones facing such an uphill task. We have the management as epitomized by the Deputy Representative, to side with us. Responsible for programme coordination and enhancing cross-sectoral synergy and results, the Deputy Representative plays a crucial role in ensuring that social protection is given due priority across various sectors and advocacy efforts. Building a joint advocacy position on social protection could be a useful strategy in developing wide understanding and ownership.

Often social-protection colleagues make important value additions to the larger programme. One can safely leverage this to promote inter-sector enthusiasm for social protection. In recent years, this value addition has resulted in smoother and more hassle-free access to the MoF. The role of the Finance Ministry is critically important as it influences sectoral budgets making them more child-sensitive. There is an important correlation between a budget that is pro-child and the one perceived as pro-equity or pro-poor. Also, a pro-child budget is often the most cost-efficient and effective in addressing human capital constraints and boosting economic growth. To be able to influence the sectoral budget, access to the MoF is considered essential. A social-protection expert inside that key office can promote this campaign much more forcefully.

In Tanzania, such strategies allowed us to achieve collaboration that proved beneficial. To this end another opportunity came by way of the Arusha Social Protection Conference. It formed the core of social protection advocacy and policy-influencing, and proved very successful. The Arusha Social Protection Conference was an opportunity created by the social policy team in Tanzania. It jelled well with the need for making social protection everyone's business. More importantly, it took the issue out of TASAF and made it a part of the national agenda.

When I arrived in Tanzania, the need for something grand and ambitious was being acutely felt. The social protection strategy had been in cold storage since 2007. The massive conditional cash transfer programme was both uncoordinated and chaotic. Though the country was implementing one of the most ambitious social protection programmes in the world, there was little recognition of its strategic potential to transform Tanzania inside out. The cash transfer programme – reduced to a numbers game of families being enroled – needed to become a powerful vehicle for development attacking both poverty and deprivation. It needed to turn into a national movement. Something momentous and spectacular had to happen. The incremental progress and nudges had to be replaced with a big, gigantic push.

In consultation with the Ministry of Finance, we decided to organize an international conference on social protection where world-renowned experts would share the best global practices, and more importantly, communicate with the Tanzanian policymakers. The conference was intended to acquire global dimensions. As the conference got a higher profile its importance for the government grew. This, from our point of view, was entirely desirable. By virtue of being the colead of the Social Protection Working Group (SPWG), the MoF was the principal organizer. This was indeed a fantastic opportunity, enough to ensure that the conference became a point of convergence for several national advocacy programmes and campaigns. This in turn mainly determined the agenda and structure of the meet and also the choice of participants, speakers and chairs for various sessions. There were three main sessions on the themes of policy coherence, inter-sectoral collaboration and monitoring and evaluation. The ministers and top bureaucrats from the departments of education, health and other social sectors became chairs and deputy chairs. Given the federal nature of the state where decision-making devolved down to the provincial and the district level, participants were drawn from different rungs of the administrative hierarchy.

Preparations and pre-conference parleys were critical to achieving success in sectoral collaboration and also for collecting meaningful inputs for the programme. Though the outcome was not exactly optimum, the meet brought the focus on Tanzania giving it a self-belief that had been missing before. The concerned sectors engaged with the event gained a new perspective on the issues they dealt with. For the first time they had greater clarity about their responsibilities and challenges. They set out to achieve their respective goals armed with a new confidence and sense of importance.

Policy Declaration

An idea popped into my head during the course of the conference that gave the event an altogether different dimension. Let me recall the backdrop so the real import of the idea could be fully appreciated. The ruling regime in Tanzania was going through a turbulent time. Elections were round the corner. The minister in charge of the meet was facing flak in the wake of an unfolding scandal. The government in general and the minister in particular were desperately in need of a morale booster, some positive news. I knew I was taking a big risk when I broached the idea of a policy declaration at the conclusion of the meet. To my surprise the response was overwhelmingly positive. Though it was entirely fortuitous I was happy with the success of my initiative.

In a region known for political turmoil, civil wars and famine, Tanzania has witnessed remarkable stability and sustained economic growth. Its GDP growth since the year 2000 has been an impressive seven per cent. One of the happening countries, Tanzania offered a sharp contrast to the spectacle of menacing tanks, a warlord's marching army and long rows of famine-stricken refugees, scenes that typified a large part of Sub-Saharan Africa until recently. A dynamic place, Tanzania had an efficient and responsive administration.

I was thrilled when the government decided to go ahead with my suggestion for a policy declaration. I shared the details of a draft declaration with the key stakeholders, especially the members of the working group on social protection on the eve of the event. This was an opportunity for coordinating with diverse agencies with all the viewpoints on the table. I conducted the consultation process and set a tight deadline. The criteria I decided for inputs had an unambiguous acceptance condition: relevance for the social protection agenda in Tanzania.

I shared the idea with the Permanent Secretary (PS), Finance, who warmed up to it. He had been very supportive of everything I had proposed during my time – a little over a year – in the country. The PS and I were almost often on the same page, and the influence and power emanating from such convergence was a huge advantage. The draft declaration was shared with the PS. That was to become a document meticulously scrutinized and approved by the government. It helped enormously that every stakeholder shared and owned the social protection agenda. Interestingly, the officials took the document more seriously than their individual sector presentations.

The last lap of the process was a three-hour discussion with the cabinet members and other experts in a room adjacent to the conference venue. Turning towards me, the Education Minister said, 'You take us through the document since you have drafted it.' Not sure whether I should be happy or worried with this remark, I started with some trepidation and went on slowly as every word was scrutinized, every sentence dissected for hidden meanings and potential repercussions. This was an exercise in policymaking involving some of the smartest people I had encountered in my professional career. They knew Tanzania's socio-economic realities as well as the legal, political and social feasibilities of the document. These politicians, highly refined and well-educated, were measured in their responses but knew exactly what their country needed.

At the end of the gruelling three hours we finalized a much pruned, two-page declaration that the cabinet approved and was ready to be signed by the Finance Minister at the closing ceremony.

Looking back, I often wonder how an idea which occurred to me just like that became part of history as far as the social-protection campaign was concerned. It came to me simply but turned big. The reward I reaped was the recognition for the validity of social protection in many distressed areas of the world. My colleagues – important figures in the bureaucracy, policy experts, political leaders and members of the media – they all woke to the transformative power of social protection and went ahead with defining it for the world.

SIX
Afghanistan

Designing cash transfer into social protection

The first thing that struck me in Afghanistan was how a well-designed UNICEF programme could still work effectively and yield results in this war-ravaged, extremely fragile social environment. *It is still possible to implement programmes to benefit people here*, I said to myself.

Long deprived of the bare necessities and in a desperate situation, the Afghans, I discovered, were looking forward to any gesture of support. It was indeed an educative experience about what it really took to get a programme off the ground in difficult circumstances. The Afghan saga started with a thought, rather an idea, and that fuelled the spurt of transformation in the mountainous country which had been through a series of armed conflicts since 1978. UNICEF decided to implement a cash transfer pilot in Mazar in northern Afghanistan – a relatively secure and stable part of the country. The idea dated back to 2011-14 when it could not be implemented but the plan was never abandoned and found its place in the next country programme (2015-19). This was when I arrived in

Afghanistan to participate in the programme at the start of a new cycle.

Within a year the pilot was implemented successfully with the benefits starting to reach the participant households. How did the situation change between 2011 and 2015? My own experience would provide some clues to the factors behind its success, which however modest, made a perceptible impact. In that chaotic situation where the writ of the government did not run far beyond Kabul, the national capital, our small success was so impressive that it topped the priority list of the social inclusion team whose entire activity was captured within the ambit of the social policy, monitoring and evaluation (SPME) concept. I had reasons to be happy, for I headed this team. The import and possibilities of cash transfers (CT) were appreciated.

The initial challenge was to agree on a design and the institutional structure. Within our organization, the agreement on the two issues was not easy to arrive at as the debate turned both fractious and contentious. Compared with our internal debate, negotiations with the government on the design were rather easy and smooth. A fierce debate went on in our office over the institutional arrangements and choosing implementation partners. The field office in Mazar and quite a number of senior section chiefs felt that given a high level of corruption within the central and local governments, the pilot had to be implemented by NGOs. The top management had similar views though they did not take a hard line.

As a proponent of the social-protection-the-responsibility-of-all campaign, the social inclusion team took a diametrically opposite stand; it insisted on routing the programme through the government. There was a whole range of lessons to be learnt from similar experiments around the world to back this argument. It did not prove difficult to convince the management about the validity of this approach. We followed it up with a dialogue with the Ministry of Labour and Social Affairs, Martyrs and Disabled (MoLSAMD). The government was willing to become a partner in the project. They were prepared and in a better position as they had recently undertaken a WB-supported cash transfer pilot. A pertinent question could be asked about the relevance of the programme particularly when a similar one was already on. While this could be a long debate it would be enough to say that Afghanistan was an entirely different situation calling for an altogether different response.

However, what was different about Afghanistan compared with the other countries where I had worked before was its isolation and absence of social coherence. A single programme could not be carried out uniformly throughout the stratified country. There was neither a donors' forum nor a technical working group for social protection. Ours was a solitary, stand-alone initiative. The World Bank pulled out most of its international staff in 2014 in the wake of an attack on the IMF campus, though they did maintain a large presence with their local staff. Decisions were, however, made mostly in Washington or Dubai where some of their social protection team members re-located after their evacuation from Kabul.

Consequently, it was not easy to collaborate with the WB. There were other issues which frustrated the need for collaboration. UNICEF intended to implement a child-sensitive cash transfer programme to promote child development while the Bank was focused on poverty reduction and income enhancement. Talks and negotiations around the design were thus intricate. What we needed to discuss first were conditional and non-conditional issues. The fact that someone was even thinking of conditionality in Afghanistan where health and education services were either non-existent or in a pathetic state, struck me as shocking. The country which had seen invasion by the Soviets, then a long spell of civil war and finally American invasion, needed healthcare before anything else. However, it had been UNICEF's experience that social services could be improved even in extremely challenging circumstances. The issue of conditionality hinged on the confidence that UNICEF with the support of line departments and partner NGOs could increase the number of schools and health centres. This was tuned in well with the work plan of the education and health sectors in Afghanistan. Moreover, countries with better social and economic infrastructure like Kenya were implementing a nonconditional cash transfer programme. In many countries it is the government which, wary of the dependency syndrome, demands conditional benefits. The Afghanistan government, however, was making no such demands. In fact, the government lacked the capacity to engage in design development in any meaningful way.

Still conditionality was put on the table. The key factor here was gender. During a visit to a village in Mazar, the social inclusion team found only boys in a community-based school (CBS). There was not a single girl child among the thirty-odd students. Enquiries revealed that the community had interpreted a government circular to mean that a CBS could enrol only 25 students. As there were well over 25 students in the village, the boys had been prioritized. Such was the level of discrimination and barriers faced by a girl right from infancy. Insights from that field trip helped us clinch the deal in favour of conditionality. Deeply discriminating gender norms could not be tackled by non-conditional programmes. At that same time we had to accommodate the demands of patriarchal tribal society to some extent.

The pilot was to be a comparative study of the two beneficiary groups covered by the cash transfer programme (one agreeing to give women and children below age 10 access to health and education services and the other declining to accept any such conditions). The latter, of course, would be encouraged to send their children to school and health camps for regular medical checkups. This was an important component of community education. The decision was a compromise that we thought was better than no programme. As it was clear one group was a little more flexible – or less intransigent – than the other. We wanted to impact both with our programme. In the end, the study became more nuanced by making a comparison between the two different approaches – something impossible to achieve in any other situation.

This was an ambitious and complicated design for any country to adopt but in the context of Afghanistan, it appeared almost adventurous. Fortunately, the UNICEF team had some bravehearts who had unflinching faith in the programme they had opted to implement. Looking back on those turbulent days in Afghanistan, one realizes that the project achieved modest success because of our recourse to soft skills and wiser counsel in that extremely difficult and complex society.

The central challenge, once the design had been approved, was to focus on capacity issues at the project site as well as in Kabul. The World Bank had recruited a team for implementation of their pilot but it was the one tasked to try out a substantially different approach exploring geographical contours. UNICEF was, therefore, required to recruit an entirely new team. While this was heavy lifting – getting qualified professionals to work in war-torn Afghanistan, with a collective determination to get the project going the new team finally took shape. The hiring was through a fairly rigorous process. Terms of reference were drawn up and advertized on ACBAR (Agency Coordinating Body for Afghan Relief and Development) the government's online procurement/HR portal. Candidates were shortlisted and interviewed, and UNICEF remained engaged throughout the process. The best available applicants were selected and the final team turned out to be very capable and committed with several of its members having prior experience in development programmes on the ground. A team was set up in Mazar. The original idea of locating the team in Charkent district, Balkh province, had to be abandoned because of the extremely poor living conditions in the district headquarters. A base in Mazar, however, was strategically important since it helped link the pilot with larger development work in Badakhshan province.

Though in theory this appeared fine in practice linking up was not easy to achieve. The provincial administration was only marginally involved in the beginning. In fact, the non-cooperative attitude of the department of social affairs in the province was extremely discouraging. While the national ministry had made available adequate office space for the project and provided management supervision, the provincial administration refused to house the pilot's district team, forcing them to rent two rooms. In many ways, this was a project being implemented in partnership with the government that had extremely limited physical assets and human resources. In the midst of a long drawn-out war the government both at the national and local levels did not have sufficient wherewithal to conduct mandatory monitoring.

In Afghanistan, I understood for the first time the true meaning of capacity. It was much beyond what the jargon literally means and was not just about the total amount or volume that could be contained or produced. It can be extended to mean the physical presence of a government. We need to understand capacity in the context of Afghanistan. This was a forbidding, hostile place where the reality of danger was much starker than that in Tanzania or Cambodia. This place was a lesson in the extremities of life.

Even when community workers, or community mobilizers were recruited for the district through the competitive recruitment process, it was an eye-opener to the powerplay within the district administration headed by a governor. The district governor objected to the means and methods deployed for the project complaining that the administration did not have sufficient information nor were there many candidates who could apply. He requested an extension of the deadline which UNICEF agreed to in good faith and in order to keep the governor engaged. Recruitment was certainly a bigger challenge than we had envisaged. We were fortunate that common sense finally prevailed and that our flexible approach worked better than a rigidly formal adherence to the rules would have.

The governor was happy that we accepted his terms and ended up offering a building for the project office. Our team moved into this rather dilapidated building close to the governor's own office in the town centre but it still had four solid brick walls.

The recruitment of community mobilizers and their retention again proved more difficult than anticipated. Every village need-ed a man-woman team. The culture ordained that they be mar-ried as per sharia law. Some had teamed up with their uncles and cousins but were rejected. Quite understandably, the pilot faced several teething problems. It was a massive effort to complete every step to move on to the next stage. And still it made no sense to pinpoint the crucible of all problems resulting in slow progress and lethargy – lack of experience both within UNICEF and the government. The project team in the district and Kabul was not immune to it either. This only meant that every small detail had to be specific and that instructions needed to cover even the minutest areas.

Personality clashes and individual rivalries also impeded progress of the project. Within MoLSAMD there were multiple factions and interest groups competing to take control of the project. Such unseemly rivalries came out into the open just as UNICEF's pilot got the ministry's approval.

An internal restructuring carried out by the newly-appointed minister required UNICEF's social protection programmes to change traditional reporting lines. It was to be channelled and managed through the new Director General of Policy and Strategy. However, this position was stillborn as the previous DG had refused to let go and still controlled staff resources. He built up resistance and engineered subversion – something very new in my experience. The government officials and particularly the two DGs spoke openly against each other. Despite strong words and grandstanding by the new DG, he was never able to gain control over the resources and the process. While dutifully following the minister's instructions, UNICEF waited for the new DG to get the project moving. As this did not happen for months, with the internal battle turning more fractious, UNICEF made a special plea to the Deputy Minister for the cash transfer pilot to continue to be managed by the erstwhile DG, whose position in the organisation was not entirely clear but who had some technical expertise and understanding of what such a project was all about.

This proved to be a smart move. The project finally took off though several problems still persisted. UNICEF had to tighten its belt and prepare for the long haul. The challenge of following the developmental principles in very fragile and poor governance conditions, and in an extremely low-capacity context, could not be overstated. There was, however, one redeeming feature amidst all this bleakness. The process of setting up the pilot did not call for the kind of massive policy-influencing exercise that would have been required in places like Cambodia, Tanzania and India. This was linked to policy work and was far less glamorous but also resource-intensive. We could not, for example, talk about impacting a million lives or even 100,000. We were concerned with at the most about 40,000. Our target audience was not the Finance Ministry or the Deputy Prime Minister but more humdrum entities like the project team, the district governor and the provincial governor. The Deputy Minister of Social Affairs was very accessible, especially when ceremonial events had to be organized – like the project launch or high-level meetings with officials in Mazar. Otherwise the social inclusion work was focused on a small pilot covering about 2000 children, an abysmal waste of resources for insignificant targets. However, unless we keep in perspective the extraordinary circumstances in Afghanistan, this may sound unkind.

Though the pilot was the mainstay of the social inclusion campaign, what was more important was an inclusive, all-embracing vision for a holistic society. And this vision had neither been abandoned nor compromised. UNICEF was keen that the country should develop an overarching social protection policy framework. That was its remit since the start of the new country programme. The country's social protection framework had largely been focused on the existing stakeholders of the MoLSAMD, i.e. the veterans, martyrs and people with disability. In the context of Afghanistan 'people with disability' is a euphemism for mine victims. Almost every day some 20 unsuspecting civilians fall victim to mines. Since it had been very patchily implemented, UNICEF wanted this framework to be based on an updated assessment and understanding of the vulnerability in Afghanistan.

It offered to provide a senior technical adviser to assist in this work of policy formulation. The first recruitment drive failed. In reality, a candidate, spotted by the ministry, had lost his original testimonials and by the time the ministry was able to issue the candidate a contract, three to four months had already been lost. The job was advertized again, just as I was leaving Afghanistan, this time for an agency rather than an individual.

The process was handicapped and obstructed every step of the way by bureaucratic interferences and fossilized rules. UNICEF was keen to follow its procedures and at the same time deferred to the government when needed. The government was often found scrambling for information while its grasp of the essentials of its own processes was poor. The situation was not helped by the government's ever-changing rules relating to seeking technical assistance and hiring staff. As a result, it kept revising its approach, adding to delays and frustrations. For example, the pay scale for technical advisers changed twice in a year. It took several weeks for the government to communicate these changes through its channels – ministries and departments – and the international development partners needed even more time to comprehend the implications.

Supporting coordination and advocacy was another key element in UNICEF's social protection strategy. This was aimed at mirroring and reinforcing the role of the social protection ministries in stable settings. Here, efficient local staff was quickly identified through competitive recruitment. They were hired within two months of advertising and started supporting policy meetings around the issue of labour. However, a divorce between policy and programme took place with the arrival of a new minister who had brought in her own team. The new Deputy Minister of Labour was also entrusted with policymaking or that's what UNICEF was told. It was logical to assume that any development regarding the social protection framework would fall within the remit of the new Deputy Minister. This was also relayed to UNICEF. Though it may seem anomalous that the officer hired with UNICEF support to look after technical coordination and policy, would attend coordination meetings around the issue of labour and manpower, the UN agency hoped that social protection policies too would be discussed across the table since they came under the Deputy Labour Minister. This assumption was not without basis.

There was a clear vision linking social protection with the ongoing work on the Afghanistan National Strategic Development Framework which urgently needed to incorporate this component. In reality, however, the process in Afghanistan was opaquer than in many other countries. Foreign embassies were playing a much more direct role, with the President's Office at the helm. The process, unlike in other countries, was not being managed by the central coordination and planning agencies like the Planning Commission in India. To be fair, there was no strong planning agency, the role having been largely allocated to the Ministry of Economy and Commerce.

The first draft we produced was impressive and had a pragmatic, forward looking approach with the right emphasis on job creation, agricultural development and social investments. There was no mention of social protection despite the fact that the government had earlier floated a major Job for Peace proposal requesting donors to pledge some two billion dollars. The Job for Peace programme included an element of social protection as in the impact of cash transfer on child nutrition. However, there was no government plan for a massive cash transfer or any poverty targeting programme. The extremely meagre resources were reserved for more pressing concerns like security, infrastructure and social services. Consequently, the policy initiatives in Afghanistan did not seem to make any visible headway. However, there were important lessons for development partners and the government to learn.

In an unstable and broken country like Afghanistan, making a case for social protection needed clarity of intent and support mechanisms. The social protection project may not take off simply because there is no physical infrastructure left intact to implement it. Hence, development programmes should look at overriding existing supply chains and services to deliver social protection schemes. Here education and health are two important conduits. Scholarships are obviously one scheme that is relatively easy to implement. In terms of an anti-poverty cash transfer, any move to establish small-scale pilots as done by the WB and UNICEF is in the right direction. However, the Bank's PMT (proxy means test) turned out to be too complex and resource-intensive to implement. There are obvious lessons here. My personal view is that it is somewhat extraordinary that the design of the pilots by both UNICEF and the WB was both complex and sophisticated, such as those designed for a stable, averagely resourceful country rather than for the one where the government machinery was virtually non-existent.

This leads us to the question about our knowledge of fragile settings. Afghanistan to my mind represents the next frontier in social protection, an issue that has just started to receive attention in that country. If social protection promotes citizens' wellbeing and state-citizen contract, then surely there is a greater need for it in environments where citizens are pushed to the brink of survival by constant conflicts or other instability-inducing factors like inadequate capacity and lack of political commitment. These problems are much tougher to grapple with than in more stable societies.

Afghanistan provides a powerful and inspiring example of setting up a social protection system in a fragile environment. Starting with a modest beginning by UNICEF and the World Bank, the country has by now been able to set up a regular, predictable cash-based social protection programme in 100 districts (one-fifth of the total districts in the country). Afghanistan witnessed for more than a decade progress marked by economic growth and improvements of key human development indicators. How did Afghanistan reach there? I have sought to explore in these pages the build-up of the political economy and the role of development partners. There might be important lessons for those in conflict and post-conflict countries.

This was largely due to the official development assistance (ODA) and the capacity brought in by the international and national development partners as well as the sizeable Afghan expatriates who returned home to take up various posts in the government. The outcome is encouraging and incontrovertible and it makes an important point that in countries mired in chronic civil war, with acute governance and capacity challenges, change is still possible. More importantly, sustained progress making a difference to the lives of millions of men, women and children can be achieved. This is a tribute to international development aid and recognition of the role it plays in extremely difficult situations. Afghanistan remains a great success story which merits more attention, elucidation and celebration.

The expansion of health and education services propelled by economic growth and significant support from the UN ensured that the future of the country would be more promising than in the troubled times when Kalashnikovs, mines, tanks and drones sought to define the magical landscape.

Progress was still possible, thanks to the wise and responsive leadership of President Ashraf Ghani, a former anthropology professor at John Hopkins University, US. A more important factor, however, was Afghanistan's fabled inner resilience. Afghan economy recovered and began to grow after the initial collapse. The economy was not the only area that had been hit during the long spell of war. Security conditions deteriorated with more districts coming under the influence or the control of Taliban and other anti-government forces like ISIS and the Haqqani network. This, however, did not deter the ambition of the central government to strengthen the macro-economic fundamentals of the country and enhance human development.

The country recently embarked on a long-term strategic planning exercise, helped largely by technical and financial support from the international development partners. The vision was clear – inclusive growth. The ambit of inclusion was to be realized largely through promoting agricultural growth and investments in health and education, the focus being on job creation. After sustaining an impressive growth rate of nine per cent between 2003 and 2013, the Afghan economy slowed to 2.7% in 2014 dipping further to 1.5% in 2015. This sharp economic decline coincided with the withdrawal of US troops from the country. A social protection system was being set up. It was here that the role of the development partners proved critical. UNICEF and the WB played a proactive, strategic role in this context.

Many positive government policies and practices do not originate in a country's strategic development planning process. They begin as pilots, as an experiment to test their relevance and effectiveness, and are then gradually given the appropriate policy space.

Lessons from Design and Implementation

1. Push the boundaries – challenge assumptions including gender-related and patriarchal ones;

2. Women are far better informed than generally assumed;

3. The desire for social protection and similar measures is strong, and providers command a high respect;

4. The local administration/government generally turns out to be a supporter as they are a direct participant or beneficiary;

5. Look for local solutions;

6. Do not rely heavily on conditionality;

7. Work in partnership with the government – let them drive the process;

8. Keep an open dialogue with the community;

9. Be prepared for high administrative cost, including the cost of community mobilization, education and targeting;

10. Find champions within the government and support them.

SEVEN
India

Social protection from ancient times

The challenge of social protection in India offers a classic case. This is a country with a surfeit of social protection programmes and schemes. One can trace the tradition to ancient times making it amply clear that the case for social protection requires no advocacy here. What is required is a reform of the existing social protection practices and programmes. While programmes have proliferated, most are notoriously mismanaged and underfunded. The case in India for consolidation, efficacy and effectiveness has been long overdue.

However, it is difficult to implement this as India still does not have an overarching social protection policy. Various initiatives are being launched in a disjointed, sporadic manner without an overall plan for the country or any of the states. This is an obvious area where India would benefit from global experience though there is nothing quite like its size and complexity anywhere else. First, let us understand the basic parameters. There are 1.4 billion people living in India, with a quarter living below the poverty line. There is another significant percentage which is very close to this line, constituting what is called 'huddling poverty'. Even a slight deterioration in their income pushes them below the poverty line. It needs no reminder that poverty is a very dynamic condition with many moving in and out of it at any given time. However, there is yet another facet of poverty – the larger area of vulnerability. According to the 'State of Working India' report,[45] 82% of male and 92% of female workers earn less than ₹10,000 a month.

The federal nature of the state and resource-sharing means that social protection schemes in India have a much more complicated architecture of resourcing, design and implementation. Change in an existing scheme requires changes centrally but also at the state level (28 states till date). The states also possess varying degrees of administrative capacity, efficiency and commitment. To a development professional it may seem like working in 28 different countries. There are several schemes which originated in the green shoots of Independence at end of the long colonial rule, like the Public Distribution System (PDS). Successive governments added new schemes, often leaving the previous ones debilitated and neglected. This led to a messy situation where confusion reigned – citizens not knowing about their entitlements, or planners without a clear picture about their targets and goals. Often, schemes remained on paper while the small allocations were mopped up by middlemen and the politician-bureaucrat nexus. Schemes were almost never closed or concluded. No government wanted to risk the political cost of upsetting vested interests that had thrived on various schemes and programmes.

Here is an attempt to deal with the current initiative to develop a sustainable policy framework. Also, we take note of the experiences and reforms within the two largest social protection schemes in India – the National Rural Employment Guarantee Act (NREGA) and Integrated Child Development Services (ICDS). There is a strong movement towards cash transfers linked to electronic IDs and bank transfers. Among the poverty targeting programmes were the two major ones – PDS and NREGA. In recent years, the PDS has been expanded to cover almost 75% of the population. There is an ongoing discussion around translating the PDS into cash-based incentives, a move which has huge implications for food security with the potential for disrupting a well-entrenched nexus of stakeholders that has thrived on the programme for almost a century. This reform, if indeed goes forward, will have to negotiate a minefield.

An overall social protection strategy will undoubtedly help. NREGA is the big success story of recent times in India. This is a fully home-grown model, built on the back of decades-long efforts towards work-based relief and poverty reduction programmes. NREGA has been a success and has provided protection from starvation to vulnerable sections of the population. The programme has undergone several adaptations and tweaking with an increasing integration of technology in payments, monitoring and supervision. While its contribution to food security and other development outcomes has been well-established, the project often has created socially and economically useful infrastructure for the community and contributed to its overall development.

It will be pertinent here to take a look at India's urban poverty since there has been a strong trend among the rural poor to migrate to the cities looking for livelihood. In response to this emerging situation, there is a determined move to replace the take-home ration scheme with cash transfers. The government is working with UNICEF and the WB in order to achieve this.

The fight against poverty and inequality has become more vocal and intense though the economic divide is growing globally. In India, the past decade has witnessed a meagre 0.75 percentage point rise in poverty reduction annually despite a stellar average GDP growth rate of above seven per cent. Against this backdrop and somewhat paradoxically, a concerted effort has been made to counter and reduce some of the more indigent forms of deprivation. Some welcome moves have been made to expand financial inclusion through Pradhan Mantri Jan Dhan Yojana (PMJDY) and other social protection programmes like ICSDS and the Targeted Public Distribution System (TPDS), not to mention legislation-based social protection measures like Right to Education and Right to Food.

In India, though rigorous systematic evaluations are lacking, initial assessment of many of its social protection instruments has shown both poverty reduction and developmental effects. The estimates for budgetary outlays vary between two-five per cent of GDP, though of late India has witnessed some worrying squeeze on social spending in areas such as the health. Having subscribed to a global agenda, countries are embarking on expansion, consolidation and reform of existing social protection measures. There is also a growing emphasis on defining the objectives of the social protection system – targeted population segments, a basket of measures – and calling for foolproof monitoring, an evaluation framework and incorporation of an attendant financing strategy.

The road to setting up a national social protection system is never an easy one, especially in a country like India that has established large-scale social safety nets and social protection programmes. Many countries such as India and the UK have enacted legislations to address the basic needs like health, education, income and food.

Many other countries are adopting what has been referred to as a 'bottom-up' approach. They have been implementing large-scale social protection programmes minus an overarching strategy or policy framework. This helps project elements of a comprehensive system like a common register of vulnerable and poor households. My view, based on experience, is that countries should adapt to ways suitable to their particular political ecosystem and socio-economic conditions with certain non-negotiable elements like basic food and income security, budgetary outlays and human development outcomes, especially targeted at the poorest.

Above all, many nations can see the need for scaling up, streamlining and strengthening these measures to reach at least six-eight per cent of their GDP, a golden mean estimated by ILO to provide a basic cover of income, food, shelter, education and health for all. For India this means an estimated increase of three-six per cent of GDP, a goal very much desirable and within its reach given its expanding national income and stagnant poverty levels.

Postscript

No picture is static. Things have changed since we struggled to persuade governments to adopt the social protection doctrine in their policy framework. Since our first initiatives social protection has come a long way to be part of the UN-mandated Sustainable Development Goals (SDGs). A government is duty-bound to set up a national social protection system and ensure coverage of the economically vulnerable. However, when it comes to meeting the goals the SP guideline is quite vague about the targets for coverage, size of budgetary allocations and benchmarking. The newly elevated status of social protection as a development strategy achieves two purposes. First, it gives the agenda a higher and more tangible profile. Today governments are more likely to know about social protection and adopt it than say, two decades ago. Unless it is a remote, inaccessible place living under the rock social protection is the new buzzword in the development parlance. Without stressing the point any further it may be said that the SDGs have contributed to the larger acceptability of social protection as a transformative mechanism. Second but more crucially, it ties in the countries with a moral imperative to track and report progress against the target set for social protection.

Impelled by the SDG targets, some kind of regional competition is foreseeable generating a faster pace of achievement. However, as evident from the target, this does not solve the two key problems impeding the policy framework of social protection either in their entirety or in any significant measure. The first still concerns its definition and therefore assumes importance. How can the countries report on something that is undefined and amorphous? They have to work out the definition of social protection which is unique to them. But how can the achievements of two countries be compared in the absence of a clearly demarcated set of parameters?

The second issue, which is related to the definition, concerns the indicators and measures of coverage. In other words, statistics about the percentage or proportion of the marginalized population that a country should aim to cover under the social protection umbrella. Even the SDG targets are vague rather than specific, leaving them to subjective interpretation with terms like 'substantial'.

Despite these limitations, the SDGs have quite expectedly contributed to a better understanding and enhanced commitment (of resources) to the social protection campaign by the governments.

Among the countries where I have worked so far, social pension has been made part of the programme in three – Lesotho, Nepal and India. These are the first countries where social protection was implemented. And it contributed to the launch of more social protection programmes, especially those with a big focus on families with young children.

As I have pointed out in the last few chapters of the book, social protection is still in its infancy. Most countries are struggling to deal with the issues the campaign throws up or focus on. The challenge is still humongous and the road is not often very distinctly laid out.

Many programmes are still poorly resourced resulting in inadequate coverage and plagued by high rates of exclusion. Very few countries are investing in developing a more efficient and refined delivery system to make the social protection programme a success. There is little investment in the management information system (MIS) or in other important areas like grievance addressing or registration and enrolment.

Often the sectors look at drivers that are distinctly physical and palpable and therefore can be counted, programmed and easily acted upon as per our body of knowledge (BoK). In the most developing countries, many sectors are still faced with a huge supply gap resulting in enrolment and completion rates far below the target. These sectors are indeed understandably focused on the numbers. Reassuringly this has begun to change spotlighting the quality of education that UNICEF insists on. An analysis of the factors leading to poor completion rates brings out other issues like student-teacher ratio, quality of teaching, teaching material and poverty. What often remains unstated is the keenness and psychological propensity of the child to earn. Quality being a two-way street, the student and their agency are equally important. It is here that social protection goes a long way in enthusing the child about their future. Strengthening demand is an important option for those in charge of the programme. They need to create a demand for education, both among students and their parents.

So, if our initial efforts are either snubbed or met with a less than enthusiastic response, we naturally tend to recede into our shells. Returning to the agencies that manage the social protection programme then remains our only choice. In many cases they are the Social Welfare Ministries. We fail to enhance our strengths and resources, and therefore are far less useful to our direct government counterparts than we could have been otherwise. Getting all this corrected within UNICEF is far more important than we initially assumed. It is indeed important to look inward.

Social protection today is an intensely alive area impacting the lot of the marginalized while bringing a whiff of spring to other parts of society. This is change on the threshold – a choice whether to postpone the renewal or welcome it.

Endnotes

[1] FAO, (2008), Corporate Document Repository, available at: https://www.fao.org/documents/en/detail/1857

[2] https://advocacyguide.icpolicyadvocacy.org/21-defining-policy-advocacy

[3] Britain's Department for International Development (DFID) was established with a mandate to meet the challenges of tackling world poverty.

[4] Learning from the Renewable Natural Resources Research Strategy, Effective Policy Advocacy, DFID, undated

[5] Advocacy Coalition Framework (ACF) of Sabatier and Jenkins-Smith (1988).

[6] Performance and Innovation Unit, UK Government, March 2001

[7] Better policy delivery and design: A discussion paper, March 2001, Andrea Lee Admiralty Arch Performance and Innovation Unit

[8] https://www.grameen.com/ Grameen Bank is a microfinance organisation and community development bank founded in Bangladesh. It makes small loans to the impoverished without requiring collateral

[9] UNDP 2005

[10] 2016 HDI

[11] The World Food Summit of 1996 defined food security as existing 'when all people at all times have access to sufficient, safe, nutritious food to maintain a healthy and active life'.

12 Economic access to food

13 WB's Bangladesh SSN assessment/stocktaking

14 https://www.ifpri.org/publication/comparing-food-and-cash-transfers-ultra-poor-bangladesh

15 Zillur Rahman made an epochal and highly significant contribution to sustaining democracy in Bangladesh. When caretaker government, stepped in 2008 to rescue the country from the internecine Bandhs, hartals and the political wrangling between Awami League and BNP, with the not so express support of the military, Rahman was inducted (and he agreed I am told after considerable introspection /reflection) as the industry/ commerce and the education minister. He implemented a tranche of long awaited reforms and finally was also instrumental in negotiating and mediating between the political parties / the civilian arms and the military for the return of the military to the bunkers and conduct of peaceful elections following which the Awami League was voted in power and Sheikh Hasina became the prime minster.

16 Bangladesh PRSP 2005- https://www.preventionweb.net/files/9305_cr05410.pdf; The PRSP outlines a national programme for poverty reduction which is the foundation for lending programmes with the IMF and the World Bank and for debt relief for Heavily Indebted Poor Countries (HIPCs). The Bank and Fund invented the PRSP to ensure that debt relief money would go to poverty reduction, and to respond to evident weaknesses in relations between poor countries and the Bretton Woods Institutions in particular, lack of poverty focus, and no country ownership of reforms.(https://Cifds.unicef.org/Filing/CIFDFormDisclosure.aspx#/ScheduleA)

17 From mid-1980s to 2002-03 GoE issued an international appeal for assistance for a case load varying from one million to 14 million (2002-03, when the beneficiary numbers peaked).

18 Relative to the control group, the PSNP beneficiaries are more likely to be food secure, and are more likely to borrow for productive purposes, use improved agricultural technologies, and operate non-farm business activities.

19 MERET or Management of Environmental Resources to Enable Transition is a community based natural resource management and livelihoods support programme aimed at 'improving livelihood and

food insecurity problems for the most vulnerable and in particular women headed households through the sustainable use of the natural resource base'. MERET utilizes food-for-work and provides technical support to help vulnerable communities to plan and implement a number of activities such as SWC, water harvesting, forestry and biological stabilization measures, crop intensification and diversification, homestead production, income generation activities and feeder roads development.

[20] Designing and Implementing a Rural Safety Net in a Low Income Setting, Lessons from 2005-2009, Will Wiseman. Primary authors were Julie Van Domelen and Sarah Coll-Black, 2010

[21] Group Theory of policy making states that policies are result of compromise between various, conflicting interests in society. This compromise is mediated by the political systems.

[22] The ACF framework suggests that beliefs of the central groups and the actors plays an important role in policy making, here policy making is being considered as a more dynamic concept with the policy undergoing transformation under the influence of the policy advice/advocacy.

[23] Cambodia's social protection strategy/ https://interactions.eldis. org/sites/interactions.eldis.org/files/database_sp/Cambodia/ National%20Social%20Protection%20Strategy%20for%20the%20 Poor%20and%20Vulnerable%20(NSPSPV)/NSPSPV%202.pdf

[24] https://www.britannica.com/biography/Hun-Sen

[25] https://blogs.worldbank.org/eastasiapacific/cambodia-poverty-reduction-shared-prosperity and https://www.kh.undp.org/content/cambodia/en/home/library/poverty.html

[26] WB report on CBD

[27] Stabilization UNUT 4 Ds and the latest from Ed Miliband. There is a case to be made for an optimal set of conditions set be available for democracy to be insisted, rolled out and insisted again. Though there is also a strong case for the dictators, benevolent or otherwise, outlive their initial purpose bringing the nation back to the brink as witnessed in Zimbabwe, Syria and Egypt. If dictators knew graceful and timely exit and allowed for progressive realisation of democracy,

the story of the world, and the post-conflict, fragile states would be different.

28 Political culture: https://www.encyclopedia.com/social-sciences-and -law/sociology-and-social-reform/sociology-general-terms-and-concepts /political-culture

29 Political culture is the set of attitudes, beliefs, and sentiments which give order and meaning to a political process and which provide the underlying assumptions and rules that govern behaviour in the political system. It encompasses both the political ideals and the operating norms of a polity. Political culture is thus the manifestation in aggregate form of the psychological and subjective dimensions of politics. A political culture is the product of both the collective history of a political system and the life histories of the members of that system, and thus it is rooted equally in public events and private experiences. https://www.encyclopedia.com/ social-sciences-and-law/sociology-and-social-reform/sociology-general-terms-and-concepts/political-culture.

30 https://asean.org/

31 ILO, World Social Security Report 2010-11: Providing Coverage in Times of Crisis and Beyond

32 Mishra, U. (2010) 'Policy advice vs. implementation: Optimization of results. A case of PSNP in Ethiopia', paper prepared for the UN Knowledge Fair on Policy Advice vs. Implementation: How to find the right positioning for UN development activities at the country level? Austria Vienna Center, Vienna, 28-30 September 2010

33 Cambodia's SP Strategy making

34 UNDG Asia-Pacific social protection issues brief, Feb 2014, https:// www.social-protection.org/gimi/RessourcePDF.action?id=46017. Even in 2014, more than two-thirds of the Asia-Pacific population presently have no access to comprehensive social protection that enables people to cope with life risks.

35 TS Eliot *Falls the Shadow*

36 https://www.odi.org/sites/odi.org.uk/files/odi-assets/publications-opinion-files/9100.pdf

[37] Exploiting the synergies between social protection and economic development, ODI, Rachel Slater, Anna McCord and Nicholas Mathers May 2014 https://www.odi.org/sites/odi.org.uk/files/odi-assets/publications-opinion-files/9096.pdf

[38] https://www.theewf.org/speakers/view/he-dr-hang-chuon-naron and https://en.wikipedia.org/wiki/Hang_Chuon_Naron

[39] Estimating Rates of Return on Social Protection Instruments in Cambodia, Maastricht University, 2013, https://www.unicef.org/socialpolicy/files/2012_rates_return_combodia.pdf

[40] Chan Sopha l- https://cdri.org.kh/author_categories/chan-sophal/

[41] PFMR https://gdb.mef.gov.kh/items/PB_Model-Cambodia-Final.pdf

[42] ASEAN integration: https://asean.org/asean-integration-report-2015-4/

[43] https://www.asean.org/storage/images/2015/November/27th-summit/ASCC_documents/ASEAN%20Framework%20and%20Action%20Plan%20on%20Social%20ProtectionAdopted.pdf

[44] This was registry of poor households identified with technical support of GIZ; https://www.idpoor.gov.kh/en/home

[45] https://m.economictimes.com/jobs/92-female-82-male-workers-earn-less-than-rs-10000-per-month-report/articleshow/65953724.cms

Acknowledgements

The list of those I need to thank for helping me with the book can run into pages. Among them are friends who directly supported me during this incredible trek and also those who have helped me grow professionally talking about perspectives, prisms and points of view.

The names coming to mind from within the UN family: my seniors Edward Kallon in Nigeria; John Mcharris, Rome; Sonali Wickrema and Mohammad Diab, Ethiopia; Rana Flowers, Vietnam; Akhil Iyer, Global Director, Polio Programme, UNICEF. They taught me a lot about policy analysis and influencing.

Thanks are also due to those friends who helped me in many other ways: Hossain Zillur Rahman, Chairperson, BRAC, Dr Anamika Shally Prasad, Amitava Chakravarty, Rafi Mohammad, Aritra Sarkar, Manoj Mohanka, Amajeet Banerjee, Sabahat Azim, Jolly Shah and Shruti Kapila.

My sisters Chhaya and Asha who were always a source of strength particularly during the trying times when I felt emotionally drained.

My daughter Saisha for opting to be a fellow sufferer sharing my frustrations in the midst of the book.

To my spouse Chris Hayes for his counsel, thoughtfulness, care and support.

And a big thank you to my publishers who believed in me and handled the book with utmost care.

Finally, and most importantly, to the communities I worked for, became part of and learnt from in Bangladesh, Ethiopia, Cambodia, Tanzania, Afghanistan and India.

25 February 2020   **Usha Mishra Hayes**
Kathmandu